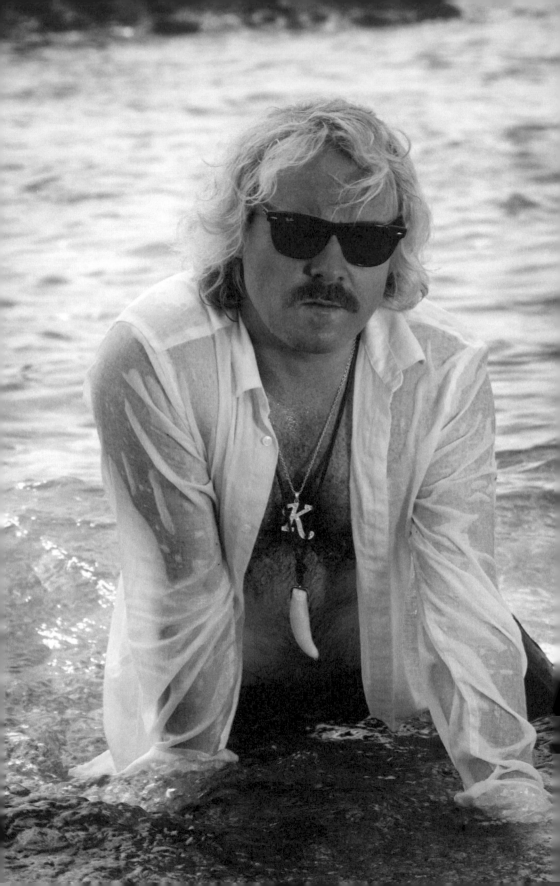

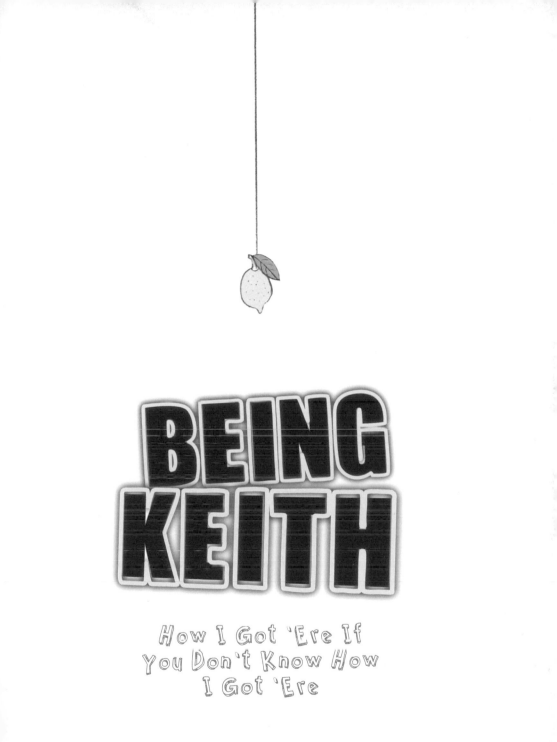

BEING KEITH

How I Got 'Ere If You Don't Know How I Got 'Ere

Author biog

Keith Lemon is a northern sex symbol. If you don't know already it's the same Keith Lemon as Keith Lemon Business Man of the Year 1993. You may have seen him on TV shows such as *Celebrity Juice, Lemon La Vida Loca, Lemonaid, Sing if You Can, Bo! Selecta* and *Keith Lemon's Very Brilliant World Tour*. As you can see he's a good looking guy and quite a hit with the ladies – from Bang Tidy lasses to stinky mingers, he's had them all.

Contents

Introduction fingy

Just got home from t' NTAs – the National Television Awards. It were the first time I've ever done t' red carpet with a girlfriend. I were quite proud when someone shouted they'd smash 'er back doors in. Rosie is lovely. She looks like a cross between someone from *Hollyoaks* and one of the fit nurses from *Casualty* and her out of t' *Office*.

Anywhere, it were a crazy night, though I were very nervous for some reason – which is very unlike me. It were a big do, like. Lovely to see Holly and Fearne. Holly's bangers looked as big as always and Fearne's nostrils looked even biggerer! We had a right laff. Fearne cudn't stop looking at me. There's no two ways about it. Fearne has got the hots for me and I fink Rosie could sense it. There were a moment of sexual rivalry in their eyes. I quite liked it to be honest.

Anywhere, it comes to the category of Best Comedy Panel Show, the category we were up for ('wc' as in *Celebrity Juice*). I had a feeling if the person that were presenting the award were somehow linked to the show, or a friend of mine, Holly's or Fearne's, then we might be in with a chance of winning. Would it be Rufus Hound? Cos he were nowhere to be seen.

F.A.F.

Not sure where he were that night. Probably out with his prostitutes. He loves prostitutes! Just kidding, dingbats!

So, on walks Russell Kane, the lovely guy from *I'm a Celebrity Get Me Out of Here!* who looks like Jedward's older lesbian sister. I know Russell, he's a very funny, lovely man and has appeared on *Juice* a few times. This were all looking good. He called out the nominations.

'And the nominations are – *QI*, *Mock the Week*, *Have I Got News For You* and *Celebrity Jews*'. I fink he meant 'Juice'.

'And the winner is... *Celebrity Juice!*'.

I saw me face in t' corner of the screen looking nervous. I looked at Fearne and had sex with her three times in me mind, then looked at Rosie and had sex with her four times, including some oral and some stuff I better not say cos she don't like me talking about it. She's the one for me... For now anywhere, as Sam Faiers from *TOWIE* were sat a few seats away from me and her bangers were crying out for some TLC – Tender Lemon Cuddles. Anywhere, where was I?

'And the winner is... *Celebrity Juice!*'

Shit me backwards, we'd won! After six series and lots of begging for votes on Twittor, we'd won t' big 'un. *Celebrity Juice,* a show on ITV2 on Thursdays at 10pm, were officially the Best Comedy Panel Show on telly. I were swallowed up in a vortex of joy (that sounds good, don't it?). I cudn't believe it. I were literally without belief. I dint even hug Rosie, which I fink I should've. (I did more than

SAM FAIERS

give her hugs when we got home that night though.)
I jumped straight up for Fearne. Even though I give her
a lot of grief on *Juice*, she's me mate and I do respect
her a lot as a beautiful woman that has to carry those
large nostrils on her face on a daily basis. Can't be easy
for her. Then I hugged Dan, the executive producer of
Juice, who is married to Holly (the spawny bastard),
nuzzled into Holly's massive bangers and approached
the stage.

I were overcome with joy and had to display me joy with
t' power of dance. Dint have a clue what I were gonna
say. I fought about me mam, me dad, me old school
friends, me girlfriend Rosie sat in t' audience, the team.
It were incredible. And what did I do? I sang two
brief extracts from the songs 'When the Going Gets
Tough' and 'Caribbean Queen' by Billy Ocean, who
I often joke is me dad. But deep down it in't a joke.
I honestly believe Billy Ocean is me dad. Ya can see
it in both our eyes.

BILLY OCEAN IS
ME DAD

Backstage at the NTAs were a total buzz, doing all those interviews and having the victory photoshoot. Mark Wright, another one from *TOWIE* seemed to crawl into our photo. *TOWIE* are like how So Solid Crew use to be. There's always one of 'em in ya peripheral vision as there's so many of 'em. They're like Gremlins!

Me, Holly and Fearne did a lot of laffing before I were whisked off back into me seat for another award that I were up for – Best Entertainment Presenter. God only knows how I got that nomination! Anywhere, Ant and Dec won it for the 11th year running and I were happy for 'em. I knew they were gonna win. I'm just lucky. I dint even know how I got 'ere. I were just riding a wave, being paid to mess about and have a laff. Now, if it were for somet like 'Best Hair', or 'Best Dressed Person' if they gave awards like that, I would've won, cos I looked Bang Tidy, even if I say so meself. But honestly, I find it hard to believe how I got 'ere. And if ya finking ya dint know how I got 'ere, well... 'ere's how I got 'ere...

I said I dint know how I got 'ere a lot then, dint I? Well, 'ere's how I got 'ere...

'Ere's how I got 'ere

I were invented in Leeds via me mam's womb. Anatomically gifted with a three-inch tally wacker, ya can only imagine how many inches I'm packing now. Said it before and I'll say it again, fick as a coke can.

I learn't nowt at school apart from how to control the mind of the female to convince 'em to do almost anyfing ya like. I'm not talking about getting her to cook for ya or do the cleaning and stuff as I'm metrosexually that way, very good around the house. I'm talking about erasicating any negative responses to sexual advances. Turnin a 'no' into a 'maybe' to a 'yeah' to a 'oh my god! There were an earthquake in me knickers!'.

Hold on! I'm just gonna look at me Twittor page. New series of *Juice* is on this week so I'm getting lots of tweets and I wanna see if Rosie has sent me a message. She's on holiday at the mo with t' girls, in Greece. I hope she don't cop off with some Greek bloke. Don't know what I'm I worrying for... She in't gonna go off with someone else. She's dating Keith Lemon from t' telly. She's winning!

OK, let's see what they're saying on Twittor...

@lemontwittor: Just been watching your dvd, your one hilarious bastard. Il be on your show one day and il abuse you.

That's nice in't it? Barry finks I'm a bastard and he wants to abuse me.

@lemontwittor bang tidy!!

That's one I get often. That and 'potato'.

@lemontwittor puberty started late on you then ha ha

Ha ha ha! Not sure what that one means...

Caprice Bourret @lemontwittor my designer at my office wants to marry u and have ur children :) xxxx

That's the actual Caprice from retro dreams' wetness! See, I know all kinds me. Ok. Let me just check if I've got a message from Rosie.

No. Nowt. Last message were 14 hours ago.

Rosie Parker @lemontwittor fought ya were being rude there and then realised you were being a different kind of rude!

That were in response to me telling her I met up with Kelly Brook, purely on a work basis. She replied 'Oh your job's so hard, in't it!' I told her it in't hard, but it would be if I were working with her – Rosie, that is. It were meant as a compliment, ya know. It's hard being with Rosie cos she's very FAF (Fit as Fuck or Flip,

dependant on how naughty you're feeling) and I get a
hard tally wacker. I fink that's how I often get away with
saying rude fings. There's always a nice motive behind
what I'm saying. Anywhere, back on track...

Little Lemon

S o, I were born, went to school, learnt nowt but had a lot of initiative, had sexual relations at a very young age and thus were very experienced in t' field of lovemeking. I knew Rosie back then as well – we met in the youthclub. But I were thirteen and she were eight so I just fought I'd wait till she got bangers else it would just be moralistically wrong. But ya just knew Rosie were gonna grow up to be fit. I knew she'd be a banker for the future, so we stayed in touch.

I were a ladies man from the day dot. I remember charging girls for snogs in the wendy house, fifty pence a snog, which back then were like five pounds. Looking back on it, I guess it's easy to see that I've always been a entrepreneurerer in the meking.

I were youngerer back then and even though I left school with no education on account of all me messing about and cos I spent most of the day trying to get off with girls, I got a job on Leeds market and soon I were owner of me own business selling Rhino Jeans. Basically, I bought a loads of jeans off this man and stuck a label on 'em and called them Rhino Jeans. Rhino as in they were right strong, like a rhino. I basically saw a gap in the market cos I fink that jeans always get a lot of wear and tear around the happy area and that's where the material goes first. I don't know whether it's just cos I've got a big cock and balls but it always goes down there for me. But these Rhino Jeans were

Me
Rosie

right tough so they'd stay strong, even for me. I've still got a couple of boxes in the spare room for memories sake. Some people would complain saying one leg were fatter than t' other, but I would say that's the style. It's encapsulating both the ragamuffin look and the emo look – which hadn't even been invented back then. The emo look, I invented that.

I lived with me mam and brother in Leeds and me family have always meant a lot to me, me mom in particular so I wanted to share a bit of the success I'd had with Rhino Jeans with her so I started saving to pay for her to get a new set of teeth. At the time they were right mashed up – like a picket fence in her mouth – so I wanted to sort them out for her. I weren't connecting meself to one woman at this stage as I had too much love in me pants for one woman.

Anywhere from Rhino Jeans I went off to Securipole which I won Business Man of the Year 1993 for. I were proper chuffed with that. And if ya don't know what Securipole is, let me tell ya what it is. It's a 2 foot reinforced aluminium shaft ya can have installed on your driveway to prevent evil scum buggers from stealing your car, or your auto-moto-vehicle as scientists call them.

And for me services to Securipole I was awarded the Business Man of the Year 1993 and that's where it all got a little more interesting. Not that me life weren't interesting before telly, it were! I've always had an interesting life.

But for now let's just concentrate on t' bits ya know me for. I'm gonna start in America because that's where I first found I had a face for telly on *Bo! In the USA*.

In the USA!

After the success of Securipole in the UK we decided to take Securipole to all t' needy people around the world. So I were over in America, LA to be pecific, trying to promote Securipole and I just so happened to be staying at the same hotel that they were filming Bo!, which were that documentary fing with those masks, that little penguin/monkey/bear fing and that ginger stalker from Transylvania who were married to his sister, the freak. It were a mad old time with all sorts staying there. Craig David, Elton John, Holly Valance to name but a few.

But let's talk about Holly Valance. Oh my god! She were Bang Tidy. I would've let her stick a digit up me and I've never let any girl do that. Me poo shoot is a deposit box only. She smelt of right nice perfume and had legs the colour of hotdogs. She wanted it, that Holly Valance. When I first saw her, she did that fing where she'd look at me too much, and she were obviously not looking at me shoes, she's gone beyond me shoes and she's looking right into me soul, via the eyes. So I said, 'Hello, my name's Keith, I've got me own business, I'm here in the United States of America promoting that business. I know who ya are, but I'd like to get to know ya more furtherer.' And she said 'I'm Holly Valance', and I said 'yes, I know that. You sang, "I wanna kiss your mouth mouth, kiss kiss your mouth"' and then we just took it from there. It's very strange that I never got off with her back then. She gave me plenty of come 'ere and back skuttle me looks. But maybe because the cameras were around all t' time. She were sunbathing by t' pool all t' time and I fink she enjoyed the admiration from

all t' blokes. She were right
nice to talk to and I still
talk to her now. She still
has that look in her eye.
When I came back from LA
I bumped into her at The
BRITs and she came over to
say 'how do!'. I fink she were a
bit surprised by all the attention
I were getting. I weren't as well
known as I am now, but I still
had Pixie Lott and Geri Halliwell
round me like flies on shit. (Did I just
liken meself to shit then?). Anywhere,
ya know what I mean! We exchanged
numbers and that were it. I'll tell ya what happened
with her later though. It's getting like *Pulp Fiction* this,
in't it? Back and fourth with t' story line. I hope I dint
forget to tell ya what happens. In case I do, I'll tell ya
now, I fucked her. Tell ya in more detail later.

Okay, so back to LA. The weather were shite. It were
cloudy a lot of the time, but I weren't there on a jolly,
I were there to work. It just so happened that I had a
camera crew following me. Nice enough lads they were.
There were this gay fella Ben, who later turned out
not to be gay (a bit of a shock) and this good-looking
fella called James, who's nearly as good looking as
me. We made a great pulling team. The cameraman,
called Pete, looked like t' little lad out of *Jungle Book*
but a grown up version with a job instead of eating
bananas all day and singing 'I wanna be like you O-oo
O-oo'. The sound recording recordist man, Joe, were a
proper gonk though, one of those techno-nonces. Knew
everyfing about computers and stuff. Turned out to be
a sound lad in the end (no pun intended!) and he later

helped me build me phone
app, Keith Lemon's Mouth
Board. He lives on a barge
now. I fink he's a sea gypsy
or a pirate. Or a tax dodger.
Only joking, Joe, if ya're
reading this. Top bloke!
Oh, and I forgot Roy! How
could I forget Roy? He
were t' oldest one out of us.
We called him 'Yoda', among
other fings, but all in jest.

I remember one night we all went to a nightclub.
Apart from me, we looked a right set of dingbats. I
had a nice off-white linen suit on from H&M. For some
reason camera crews all wear t' same sort off clothes:
army shorts, Abercomby and Fish, which is just Gap
clothes all broken up. They wore North Space a lot as
well. All dress t' same they do. We looked too old to be
in there, again apart from me. Just a bunch of English
dingbats. We all adopted American accents so people
could tell what we were speaking about. Joe's American
accent were ridiculous. Like Kermit t' Frog's granddad
or somet.

Anywhere, we were meeting Jack Osbourne inside the
club. Not quite sure how that happened, I fink t' crew
must have been filming with him earlier in t' day with
Avid Merrion. Once at t' door we just had to say 'six
English blokes', that's what name they had down on
t' door for us. Soon as we went in, one of the cameramen
Dave went straight off on to t' dance floor, quite well
spoken he were.

DOT AND KIRSTEN

'Excuse me gentlemen, I'm going off to have some fun.'

Tell ya what, he wun't have got through t' finals of Davina McCall's dance fing on Sky. They'd have just said live on t' telly, "Ere mate, fuck off!'. Funny moves he had, but he were definitely enjoying himself. I showed him how to dance proper later on. We met Kirsten Dunst from *Spiderman* in there. She were fit, but not a very sexy dancer, dint express herself in a positive manner. Bit hunched, like how I imagined Dot Cotton to dance.

We met Paris Hilton in there too. I'd have a go on her. I bet she's proper dirty. I've seen her sex tape. She did a good job! Lindsay Lolan were there too. Fit for a ginger bird! Anywhere, in case you're wondering, I got off with a few people people in the club. I can't remember their names, just faces. They all look the same, like they're all out of *Sweet Valley High*. We dint have too much of a late 'un cos I had a meeting the next day with a bloke called Fabio early in t' morning and they wanted to film that. If ya dint know who Fabio is let me tell ya who he is, or just show ya a picture.

The mojo maestro

I n t' 80s, Fabio were t' face of many love romance
novels. He is the mojo maestro. He looks a
bit like He-man and has biggerer tits than Holly
Willoughbooby. I fink he later went on to not only
be on't cover but write romance books himself, with
such titles as *Pirate, Rogue, Viking* and *Champion*.
Anywhere, he's also been in a few films – *Dude,
Where's Me Car, Spy Hard* and *Zoolander*. In the
United States of America he's also known for being in
t' 'I Can't Believe It's Not Butter' ad on t' telly. And a
goose flew into his face while he were launching a new
rollercoaster in a theme park called Thor. He looks a bit
like Thor as well. Which made him the ideal celeb to be
the face of me Securipole campaign.

He's not very well known in t' UK but massive in t'
United States of America. Women throw 'emselves at
him. He's a bit like me. So I rock up to his gaff and a
lovely place, it were. Dint know what to expect.
I wun't sure if he'd wanna get involved in the project
or not. Some people in the United States of America
cudn't even understand what I were saying, but Fabio
in't American, he's Italian and I've been out with an
Italian bird so I knew a bit of t' lingo. They eat pizza
don't they? I knocked on t' door. He answered, and I
gotta say, it were like looking in a mirror, apart from
I looked a bit youngerer, me hair were a bit shorterer
than his and he dint have a tash – other than that it were
literally just like looking in a mirror.

He asked me in and he were right nice. Not what I expected at all. We clicked straight away and were soon talking about our sexual conquests, just two blokes talking about shagging birds. Proper man's man, he were. He showed me around the place and it were like somet out of *Cribs*. Kinda place ya dreamed of having. His plasma weren't as big as mine though. His were 60" and mine's 62". But his speaker system were outta this world. Four fuck-off speakers as big as me mam's front door. Bet they threw off some wattage. They had a kind of mixing desk to work 'em that were like somet out of *Superman 3*. Ya know the one with Lionel Richie in it. Were't Lionel Richie? Not sure, anywhere. That big computer that takes over t' world and mekes all traffic lights fight. The one where the green man on't traffic lights has a fight with t' red man. Oh I know who it were! *Not* Lionel Richie, but Richard Prior!

So, Fabio took me to his garage. His hobbies include a passion for off-road motorbikes and he wanted to show me 'em. All 365 of 'em! Cudn't believe it. Christ knows how he gets one out from the back of garage. He proper loved 'em though. He got one out and showed me a few wheelies. He let me have a go on one, bearing in mind I crash anyfing with an engine me. Apart from cars, vans and stuff, I've crashed a snowbike in t' past and a few motorbikes. Anywhere, I get on this little fing, probably made for a six year old. All's going well and suddenly I lose control and crash into some bins, in America they call 'em 'trashcans'. I fink 'that's fucked it'.

He's not gonna be part of me Securipole campaign. I were 'ell bent on getting him, as well. He were perfect. Women love him; men wanna be him. He were the perfect face for buying into the Securipole lifestyle. Plus, he weren't gonna be too expensive cos I'm sure he just wanted the exposure in t' UK.

I told him I were sorry and he said he'd fink about the campaign. He were worried he fought it were gonna come across a bit gay. Him being half-naked, holding a pole covering his knob. I assured him it weren't gay but sexy and the idea were to attract a female audience, but still keeping it manly. That's why it were a right clever idea. So, he said he'd sleep on it, but offered to take me out that evening. Now, I fought *that* were a bit gay. But then he said we'd be going out to get some minge. Well... he dint say 'minge' he said 'pussy'. But by the end of the time he spent with me he were calling it 'minge' and learnt lots of other youthermisms. Such as 'bangers and gash', 'ham sandwhich', 'mouse's ear' and many, many more.

Ooof! I've got shooty arse. Gonna go for a poo and call it a day. I'll write a bit more tomorrow. Just check if I've had a tweet fing from Rosie... No nowt. I wonder if I'll still go out with her when I've finished this book? Who knows, I could be shacked up with Kelly Brook. Super fit. I'd let her kick the crap out of me. Oooosh! I once had a dream about her and there were two of me. She sorted both of us out no problem. Can't believe I actually know her in real life. She's a lovely lass. Imagine if she were ya bird though. Every time ya left her stood at the bar there'd be blokes chatting her up. That's why it's nice wee Rosie's fit, but not insanely fit cos she's not got much in t' way of bangers. Similar to Fearne Cotton in some respect. Imagine if me and Fearne got it together. That might be good for me career. Fink people would like to see us together. We could do the *Hello, OK* magazine shoots maybe. Perhaps I'll ask her one day. I'll wait and see if Rosie tweets me. If there's nowt by 10 o'clock, I may ask Fearne out tomorrow. Me Nando's card an't expired yet. I could take her there. See ya in t' next chapter. Good this in' t it. It's very ferapeutic. Wish me computer had spellcheck on it though.

How do! I'm back! Had a crazy few weeks so I an't had time to write nowt. But just to fill ya in... Rosie did tweet me back. I knew she would. And when I said she weren't insanely fit, I were lying. She is! I fink this could be the girl that gonna be the cure to all those STDs. Joking! I always wear rubber johnnys. So anywhere, as I'm writing this I'm proper ill me. I'm freezing but sweating laid in bed watching *Tootsie*, Geena Davis and Jessica Lang were fit in that film. Love those naughty 80s birds.

Rather than just jumping straight back to the United States of America, I'm gonna give ya a brief summary of what I've been up to and then I'll get back to where we left off. When I were in mnsjwjndjksmkldmdsmmm boooooo""""""""""""""""""""""""""""""" .

Sorry! I nodded off on me keyboard. See, I'm proper ill me. So quickly, in t' past few weeks I've started me new show *Keith Lemon's Lemonaid*, which is for ITV1 Saturday nights . When I say 'nights', I mean just before *Britain's Got Talent*. I'm gonna have to get off me effs and jeffs out before I go on. We've started the seventh

series of *Juice* and got our highest ever ratings but I've been busy in and out of the edit for t' film.

By the time ya're reading this ya should know that I've got a film out, that's *Keith Lemon: The Film*. I can't tell ya how annoying it is that people keep saying, 'couldn't ya fink of a title?' Yeah... the *title* is *Keith Lemon: The Film*. What were t' Spiderman film called? *Spiderman*! What were t' Batman film called? *Batman*! Maybe we should call the film *The Amazing Keith Lemon* like that new Spiderman film reboot fing. Was good that.

OK! Let's get back to it. America! Back when they were filming *Bo! In the USA*, I fink that were the first time I'd ever been to the United States of America. Not many people could understand what I were saying while I were over there. I fink that's why I had a connection with Fabio. Nobody can understand him either. Cos I guess in the United States of America me and him are foreign. I like LA for a booze up but I don't fink I could live there. There's no centre to it, ya know like a town centre, and they don't really have proper pubs like, they don't even seem to like pubs. Madness! But it were handy that I made pals with Fabio cos he showed us round and stuff. When I weren't hanging out with Fabio trying to get him to be the face of me Securipole campaign, I'd go shopping and I found some good shops on Melrose Place , which to be honest I dint know were a real place. I fought it were just a telly show back in t' 90s. But ya can get some good clobber down there.

Sometimes I'd sit by t' pool and just look at t' birds. Well, I say birds, there weren't that many apart from Holly Valance, but she were Fit as Fuck. Sometimes I'd watch 'em film their *Bo' Selecta* fing. Proper mad. I remember I went with t' crew to watch that pervy little

bear with t' dick interview Jenny McCarthy. I had her
Playboy issue when I were a young lad. I wanked off to
her one day so much that nowt came out. It were like
the end of me tally wacker just coughed, looked up and
said 'No more! No more! Go out and meet people!'
I fink all teens go through that stage of constantly
wanking. It's like a new toy in't it? A new toy that dint
need batteries.

So anywhere, cos the bear were sweating a lot cos
it were hot (I were hot and I'm not covered in fur),
they built a marquee over where he were gonna be
interviewing Jenny McCarthy. She turned up and
she looked just as fit as she did in me jazz mag I had
when I were a young lad. She were on good form, too,
considering she'd already done 40-somet interviews
that morning. She were promoting her book about how
to be a mam or somet. It were hard to listen to her while
she were titmotizing me with her big LA bangers. The
bear and her were having a flirt off. She won the flirt
off when she went down on him and sucked his little
bear knob though. It sounds like I'm meking it up, don't
it? But they put it all in t' show. Ya can see it with ya
own eyes. My she were fit. A stereotypical Bang Tidy
American beach babe!

They started off just filming me meetings with Fabio
and then they started wanting to put *Bo' Selecta* people
in me bits. I fink that's what they do with reality shows
and documentaries and stuff. They meke shit up dint
they so it's more entertaining for t' viewer? Like that
TOWIE programme. That's not real is it? *The Vampire
Diaries* is more realistic than that show.

One day they had me doing
a scene with Craig David,
but he were dressing as that
scary Rabbit from *Donny
Darky*, ya know that film?
It were very odd like. They
also had me with Emma
Bunton. She were playing a
psychiatrist. I know Bunton
in real life now. She's one
of me mates. Lovely bird.
Drinks like a tramp.

It were good doing those
little acting bits that weren't
real. I fink that's what gave
me the bug for t' telly game. Me brother always said
it were show business I were destined for, rather than
t' security business. In fact, on subject of 'R' kid. I
remember we did a scene recreating 'R' Greg coming
out. Me brother's hormone sexual, as I said. It weren't
how it actually happened. I fink that'd be too rude to
put on t' telly. He got caught out rather than coming
out. But in t' show they had him played by *Some Chips
and a Pint of Lager*, Will Mellor. Or if you're American,
Will Mell–OR. Nice bloke. Well, he were playing
Gregory – and Cleo Rocos were playing me mam. Have
to glamourise it for t' telly dint ya. Mam, I'm not saying
ya aren't glamorous but ya dint look like the funny lass
from Kenny Everett, who often had 'em half hanging
out. Lovely Cleo Rocos.

I remember the clothes that I wore in that scene.
They were actually mine from t' 80s. The scene were a
backflash see. We were having our dinner and Gregory
were trying to tell us that he were hormone, which is

not actually the way it happened, as I said. I remember I were working late and when I came home I caught him in t' kitchen with another man. He always said he weren't sure but I told him, man on man, means ya are. You're hormone! I'm quite liberal me, I like all kinds. I've always said that one animal is different to another animal but they're all animals and they all have to eat nuts so they're all on the same plane really. And since he has come out he's been happierer ever since. I knew he were troubled with somet before he admitted it. He's not with t' same lad but he's got a new fella and he's a top bloke. Gregory's got aspirations of being a dancer. I'm not sure if it'll ever happen for him. He's a bit tall. It's good that he sticks out when he goes for auditions but I don't fink he sticks out for t' right reasons. He can dance though! Us Lemons have all got the dancing jean, I fink. Ya may have seen me dancing on't telly, I've got some moves!

LOVELY CLEO ROCOS

Checking up on R Gary

I were in LA for six weeks. We shot me ad campaign with Fabio, but I weren't allowed to air it in t' UK. They did show it in t' programme *Bo! In the USA* though. Shame it dint come off proper. I fink it would've really put Securipole on t' map. Anywhere, I made some good friends there, and I've been back since.

To be honest, when I finally came back to the land of the Lemon it were a bit of a comedown. From the sunshine of La–La land to the pissing down rain tapping on me porta-cabin roof. That's where I use to run Securipole from, a porta-cabin. It were grim . We've got proper premises now like. I don't work there much any more though, 'R' Gary runs it. Gary's me cousin. I just own t' company.

Aye, I've come a long way from that porta-cabin in Leeds, when I won Businessman of the Year 1993. That were a proud day. I met t' Lord Mayor of Leeds back then. I know they're just a normal person wearing a big chain around their neck and I'm sure I'd be more chuffed if I'd met Mr T, but back then it were like meeting the King of Leeds! I say the King, but it may have been a woman. Can't remember now. Honestly it were a big moment though. Anywhere, I fink it were that time in LA that gave me the push to do telly. So that's when I got me finking cap on. How could I get me some of that telly action again? There were no one on telly like me. OK, Owen Wilson looked like me, but he were Hollywood. He were big screen. I wanted that

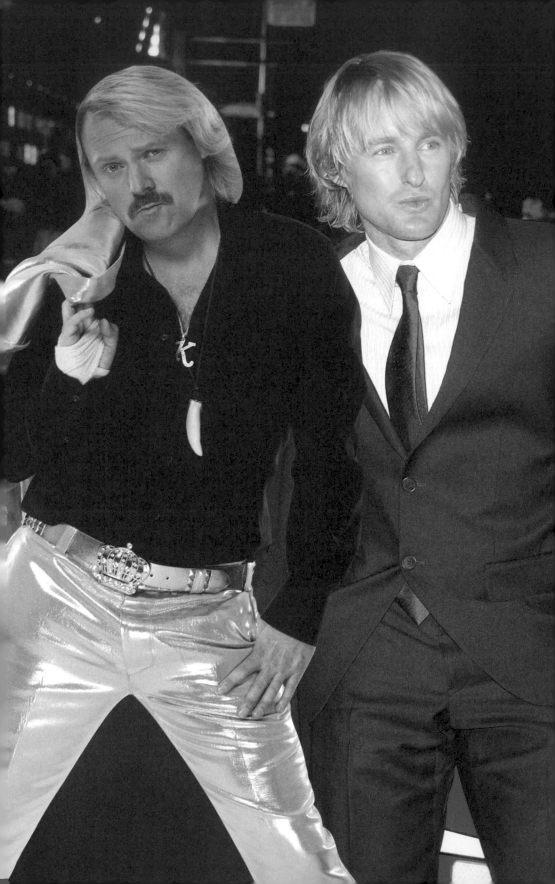

small screen, to be in t' corner of every room in t' United States of England. Then I'll have a pop at t' big screen later!

How do! Had a break from writing for a couple of days. Were too poorly. Ya fought I were poorly in t' last chapter, dint ya? Well, I got worse. I bet ya fink men like me don't get ill. I've got earache now. Doing me 'ed in, in't it. Feels like I'm under water. Maybe I should have me ears syringed? Ya ever had that done? It's amazing! Feels like the best shit in ya life. It's like an orgasm and a good crap all at the same time! Were shooting *Celebrity Juice* t' other night while I were still ill. Had to get a bit drunk to numb the flu feeling and it worked. We had Jason Donovan on. What a lovely bloke! Proper threw himself into the Juice World and were proper daft for two hours. He also admitted that he'd had a go on Kylie ... Lucky, lucky bastard!

Footballer Robbie Savage were also on. He's got bea-u-tif-ul hair, nearly as nice as Patsy Kensit's. Gotta call her to meet for lunch to talk about doing somet together. I'm always dreaming of doing somet with her... Always had a fing for Patsy.

Me best mate from Sheffield were on *Juice*, Gino D'Acampo. Were a good show! They dint show Rosie sat in t' audience though. She said she were glad, but I fink deep down she wanted to be on telly to brag to her mate, Hannah. I've never met Hannah. I bet she's right fit – and that's why Rosie's never introduced me to her.

Yesterday I were at a Q&A fing about this book. It were at BAFTA. Me editor, Jane, were interviewing me. She'd like a bit of Lemon, I can tell. I fink I can see t' desire in her eyes. She did a good interview though. Got onto the subject of Rosie. I could see disappointment in her face that I were hooked up. I were telling her how me and Rosie met. I've known her years – since she were about eight and I were 13. I dint go there then though, but I knew she were gonna grow up to be a sort. And as soon as she did I 'sorted' her a couple of times. It's a bit serious now, but I'm enjoying it. I can totally be meself with her. She knows that I look at other birds and flirt with 'em but I never stick owt in. Anywhere, back to the whens and wheres of me career...

The Very Brilliant World Tour

S o I'd taken **Securipole** to the United States of America and delivered it to the masses, came back but I'd caught the bug for being on t' telly from my guest appearances on *Bo!* So, I put some of the bits that I'd done on that *Bo! in the USA* programme together on a DVD and sent 'em to ITV2 with an idea for a holiday show. Ya get paid to have a right good holiday and a laff. What better telly idea than that?

Anywhere, a bloke called Zai Bennett got back to me and I went in for a meeting. I took him a little gift of some *Nuts* magazines. I remember one of the issues had Lucy 'Big Tits' Pinder on t' front. It may have been the first time Lucy Pinder had her nips out. For ages she kept 'em covered. We looked at those mags for a while before chatting about me telly idea. So, we did a bit of male bonding over some lovely jugs, and then we got down to business. My new mate Ben from the Bo! programme were with me. We put on a clip of me with Fabio, when I went to his house and he let me have a go on his little bike. I told Zai that's what I wanted to do. Not fall off bikes – I'm not a effing stunt man – but go around and meet people in different countries. He saw straight through me though and said:

'What ya want is for us to pay ya to go on holiday?'

I laffed and said, 'Yeah.'

I always find honesty is the best policy. If a girl is fit and ya wanna finger blast her, ya should tell her. If ya don't, ya might miss out. But it's all about timing. If ya want some more pulling tips like that, ya should get me last book, *The Rules*. You'll be reeling in the high class totty before ya know it. So, anywhere, I laffed a bit longer, then asked Zai:

'D'ya wanna do it then?'

He said: 'Leave the *Nuts* magazines with me and I'll get back to ya.'

So, I did. Two weeks went by and then we got it, t' green light! I were gonna be doing me own telly show, in which I just went around world. I cun't believe it! I were proper chuffed.

So, I set out a flight plan in the shape of a shark. Sharks are exciting and it were gonna be exciting! I were excited! Mexico, Japan, Las Vegas, Egypt, Iceland, Australia. One of those gap year fings like posh students have. Take a year off and just go bumming around t' globe. In fact, that's what it were originally called, *Keith Lemon's Gap Year*, but ITV2 fought it sounded too studenty. And I spose it did. But they wanted to call it *Keith Lemon's World Tour*, which I fought suggested I were a stand-up comedian, which I'm not. I don't tell jokes and I don't really laff at 'em. When someone tells me a joke I just fink they're clever riddles. So, I fought OK, if it's gonna be called 'World Tour' it's not just gonna be any old world tour, it's gonna be brilliant. So that were it, the title – *Keith Lemon's Very Brilliant World Tour*. But the title were so long that when it came up on the Sky menu, it just said: *Keith Lemon's Very Brilliant*. Which I liked betterer.

But before I did me own new show I got offered the chance to host *Big Brother's Big Mouth* – the show that Russell Brand use to host. I use to know him before he moved to the United States of America. I an't seen him in years. I can remember I use to take t' piss out of his ladies jeans. He said: 'You'll be wearing these one day, Lemon.'

I said: 'I effing won't!'

OK. I wear tight jeans now, but they don't belong to lasses. Anywhere I don't buy 'em, me stylist Heather does. Yeah, I've caught London. I've got a stylist. Ha-ha, me, having a stylist. Heather knows what she's talking about, though.

Anywhere, *Big Mouth* were gonna be a new experience for me and I had some big pointy shoes to fill in the shape of Russell Brand's feet. It were my first proper job on telly and it were live! I had a good time on *Big Mouth*. The team were lovely – one girl in it pecifically were really nice. Blonde she were. And when we were about to go travelling she gave me a bum bag, or if you're American, a fanny pack, and it had a little keyring on with a picture of her. I can remember she said she'd never given a blow job and I said 'ya can give me one if ya want, and ya can use me as a tool to practice on, so when ya fall in love with whoever ya're gonna fall in love with, you'll know how to give head'. So, I'm generous that way. I would often bump into t' Bang Tidy Davina McCall too. Davina is lovely, just like ya see on t' telly. She's right sexy, too. When she looks at ya, she just looks into ya soul. I'd smash her back doors in, but she's a good friend. A lot of people fink that I'm a right womanizer, but I've just got a lot of lady friends, that's all. I like hanging out with birds too. They

Shark-shape flight plan

seem to connect with me. I fink it is because I'm like a locket – hard on t' outside and soft on t' inside. I'm a good listener. Listen to this... apparently Will Young is hormone sexual. Would've never seen that, me.

So anywhere as soon as *Big Mouth* were finished, we planned out what we were gonna do in each country for me programme – and me, Roy, Ben, James and Joe set off to our first destination for *Keith Lemon's Very Brilliant World Tour*, Japan!

I went home to Leeds to say 'Ta-ra!' t' lads and tell 'em the great news that I'm gonna have me own show. Dint fink they believed me though. Had a right good Sunday roast at me mam's, who were very excited about me trip. And finally, I made sure R Gary had everyfing under control back at Securipole HQ. Then I came back to London and the following morning – so early I still had a stiffy in me pants – I set off t' airport to fly to Japan, home of the inventors of egg fried rice. (Or so I fought then...).

Not guilty

In the land of the non-egg fried rice

If you've never been to Japan, ya may have seen it on t' telly in that Bill Murray film *Lost in Transfusion*. In accordance with its location, Japan is situated on the shark's tail rudder on me map or if you're touring the world following a shark-shaped flightplan.

Before I went to Japan, the fing I could picture in me mind is what I'd seen in London's China Town. Lots of Chineses walking around and little orange ducks hanging upside down in restaurant windows. But it's not like that at all cos the people in Japan aren't even Chinese, as it turns out – that's in China and Hong Kong. The people in Japan, they're Japanese and if ya fink they're t' both same ya being racist and ya wanna get over yaself and recognise it. It's far too easy to call somet that's not the same as ya names, and I'm not about negative shit. If that's what ya about, then ya can stop reading this right now.

Anyway, quick fact for ya, they say that the 'pan' element of the word 'Japan' derives from the word frying pan which is what Japanics used to wear on their heads before hats were invented. Me tour guide that tour-guided me round Japan were called Yujiro and I'm still in touch with him to this very day. In fact, he emailed me t' other day to tell me it were snowing there. I dint fink it snowed there. Apparently ya can go skiing in Japan! How effed up is that?

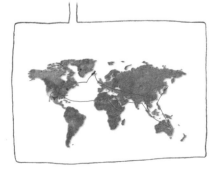

Anywhere, I weren't as intelligent back then as I am now so I cudn't say words as good as I speak 'em now, so I just called Yujiro 'Glenn' – as he looked a little bit like Glenn Medeiros from t' 80s, who sang 'Nowt's gonna stop me love for ya'. (He dint really look like him, but he did have arms and so did Glenn.) Top bloke Yujiro Glenn were. He also reminded me of me old mate at school Dereck Tooteager, who were a bit Japanese as it happens, but more like Eskimo.

First place he took us were a market called Ameyoko market. It were good. I ate all sorts or weird shit that in t' past I wouldn't never've put in me mouth. But I were there to have fun, do stuff I wun't normally do and fatten me horizons. It were there where we teached each other about day-to-day phrases that each of us use in our own countries. I told Glenn 'Bang Tidy' meant 'fit bird' or if somet looks good like. I told him it can also mean 'sexy'. He told me that 'sexy' in Japanese is 'sexshy'.

After the market, we dressed up as Monkey Magic. He were Tripitaka from t' telly show in t' past *Monkey*. I use to watch it when I were a kid. It were about a Monkey Ninja that flew about on a pink cloud. Mad as fuck, it were. Anywhere, this were the norm at Harajuku. Which apparently is the fashion mecca of Japan. It's a bridge where crazy bastards dress up. It's a lot of fun as I like dressing up, me. There were this one man that fought he were half-man, half-cat. A mad cat twat, if ya ask me. He were doing all these cat moves and licking himself. Not me cuppa tea, but each to there own, I say.

One day I remember we went techno-shopping, cos Japan is also the home of technological advances. It's very advanced in the realm of gadgetry. We found

IN THE LAND OF THE NON-EGG FRIED RICE

Fuji rock festival

this little robotic dog. Now, this were a few years ago ya gotta remember, but it were good. I fought it'd be a great tool to help the minds of kids who had no minds – or dingbats. I'm always finking how I can help others, I am. So, I bought the dog with plans to also buy the rights to it, and took it to the Fuji Rock Festival so I could get some quality pop/rock acts to help me come up with a theme tune to help promote the dog as a mind development tool for kids. Well, the responses were amazing! I'd written the lyrics meself and planned to get Juliette Lewis and the Kaiser Chiefs to sing the song for the ad selling the dog. It went somet like this...

Little Child
So Tender and Mild
But with the strength of an ox
You had a real dog
But you crushed him to Death
Now he's Buried in a box
But don't worry now you got a new Friend
He barks and he begs
There'll be no tears
When you Rip off his ears
Or Break his tiny legs
His tiny legs!
Cos he's more better
Metaller
More indestructibiller
Conan the Artificial dog
–For over passionate kids that
    Kill their pets cos they're slow.

That were the slogan, catchy right?

I fink Juliette could feel how passionate I were about the project and congratulated me with a touchy-feely cuddle. It were lovely. She's a crazy bastard, but a lovely one. The Kaiser Chiefs were good lads to. Well, they're from Leeds, aren't they?

Since then the robotic dog hasn't gone anywhere. I couldn't get enough support to get it off the ground. But we did sell a calendar which raised money for autistic dogs. We got autistic dogs to paint pictures, and the more autistic these dogs got, the better they got at painting. I'd put the paintbrush in their mouths and they'd just paint. And some of those paintings were just beautiful, like I'd never seen. Better than Neil Buchanon on *Art Attack* could ever do, or even the man who replaced Neil Buchanon. Better than *Mister Meker* on CBBC too, yeah these dogs were really good. Some of these dogs dint even know they were dogs and would behave like other animals, it were horrible to watch. So, we raised a bit of money for that. I couldn't get any celebrity to promote the calendar so I just sold them on the street and from door to door.

I've always been an animal lover. Trust me the ladies love it if ya go a bit soft over animals, specially when ya combine it with a bit of charity.

Anywhere, while I were in Japan, I met Bruce Lee's brother, Dairy Lee. Great singer. Later in t' evening, I met up with Tamzin Outhwaite from *EastEnders*, *Red Hat* and some other drama fings on t' telly. After romancing her on a boat after a sushi dinner, I took her back to me hotel. I were staying in one of those little cubicle hotels. There weren't much room in there for both of us so we did get close. And if ya were wondering what she were doing over there in t' first place, I'd flown

her over as I fought she'd be a nice bit of eye candy for t' programme. The next day she went back to the UK bow-legged after a night of passion with me in the cubicle, and I stayed in Japan and got all cleansed at a Buddhist temple before attending the international birdman rally. That's where people bring their mechanical flying machines they've made in order to jump off a cliff to win a trophy. I got it a bit wrong though and dint win any trophy. I turned up in a Bernie Clifton Emu costume.

I immersed meself so much in Japanese culture that I almost felt Japanese meself, accept I cun't speak the language.

Ooooof! Me ears are really aching. Gonna put some eardrops in. Ey up, I've got a text from Patsy Kensit. She were just asking me dates for shooting extra scenes for me film. Were hoping she were texting for a date. I'd go out with her, but I wun't do nowt. Not while I'm seeing somebody already. Honest, Rosie.

Right. I'm off out in a bit. Gotta go to a premiere of a Lionsgate film cos they're showing the trailer of me film at the beginning. So exciting!

How do! It's me again. So I last told ya about me trip to Japan. We were there for two weeks in total. Came back to London to pack different clothes and have me hair trimmed and then we set off to the United States of America!

Gonna tell ya about what happened in the United States of America very soon. But let's have a little catch-up first and let me tell ya who and what I've been up to more recently. I've been busy as a shitting dog filming me new telly show, which is gonna be on at 6.15pm on Saturdays which is very early for me. Hope I don't say 'piss', 'shit' or 'fuck' too much! If I do they can just cut it out though; it's not live, and anywhere, I have a swearbox that I pop on me 'ed if I feel a naughty coming on. The show's called *Keith Lemon's Lemonaid*. You'll know this by now as it'll already have been on t' box by the time you're reading this. In it, I spit in the face of people's problems and meke their dreams come true. I am the Dream Meker. Oh, and I've been working with Adidas. Who'd have fought it? Me being t' face of Adidas. Only sport I do is swing ball. Three hours of swingball a day though. Ya need to work for a body like this. They keep sending me clobber, as well! Sent me an ace gold biker jacket with wings on t' back! I wun't wear it to go shopping like, good for t' telly though. I like jazzing it up for t' telly.

All still going well with Rosie. In fact, we've been shooting our own reality show. She's moved down to be with me in t' Big Smoke. When she first moved down she were in my flat and there just weren't enough room, it were a small pad. And she weren't happy with just one drawer, and she cudn't have the wardrobe cos it had all my clobber in. And I've got loads of clobber. So we had to move to a new place. It's quite a nice normal place.

Odd living with a girl when I'm use to me own space. But it's going well. I've got blow jobs on tap and she's a great cook. She's told me not to mention too much of our sexual exploits in this, but she won't mind me telling ya I'm getting the odd blowy. That's why they give ya 'em. So ya tell people. I fink it's like a dog marking its territory. It's their ownership on ya. The only problem is that bloody programme *Sex and the City* is on constantly. I don't like that programme. It gives women too many ideas, it mekes them all independent.

So where were we in the narrative of the story – oh, yes, the United States of America!

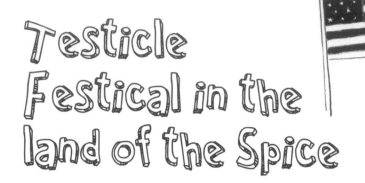

Testicle Festical in the land of the Spice

I fink, like most kids from me generation, I always loved the United States of America as a kid. It seemed a place where dreams could come true and Spiderman lived there and the A-Team. I'd been before as ya know, but I'd never been to Las Vegas and that were our first destination in t' United States of America. Las Vegas is basically the shady side of the American Dream and features an array and an abundance of spectacles to pleasurise your sensories. I remember we arrived smack bang on the shark's hooter early in t' morning like 1am or somet. It were still hot and the heat wolloped the back of me neck as I got out of t' car. The place we were staying were a lot posherer than I expected it to be. I were proper excited cos I knew some of the stuff we'd planned to get up to. I were gonna be hooking up with one of me old friends, Mel B, aka Black Spice, and the plan were to get up her! Fit!

First up, we filmed a little tour of the place. The streets were pathed with pissed-up party people holding glasses filled with brightly-coloured cocktails that looked like bongs full of booze. It were a total totty nest. Like Blackpool with a thousand times more lights. I knew I were gonna like it 'ere. We'd arranged for me to join t' Chippendales, who if ya don't know who they are, I'll tell ya who they are. They're a dance troop of strippers that were well known in the 80s, mostly for

taking their clothes off, but are still going strong today. A bit like the fellas in that film *The Full Monty*, but better looking and youngerer, in fact some of 'em were honestly as good looking as me. One of 'em looked like a youngerer Fabio. I bet he were a right fanny magnet. It was good fun for all the family because they din't reveal their peniseses or owt.

Anywhere, they seemed like a good bunch of lads and after an hour or two of going through the routine, I showed 'em what I'd brought to wear for that night's performance. I fink I'd left a bit of it at home cos there only seemed to be some blue boxing boots and a pair of blue rubber pants that dint really hold in all me tally wacker, so me nib and a left knacker hung out the right side. They said it were a bit inappropriate and lent me one of their costumes, which consisted of a long *Matrix*-style coat, cuffs and collars, a bit like what a male Playboy bunny might wear.

I'd put Mel B on the guest list. I hoped she dint stand me up. I were really looking forward to showing her what I were made of. She did turn up, even if she were a bit late, but that's Mel B, she's always late. I fink she were suitably impressed by me performance with t' Chippendales even though I forgot half the routine. Good job I'm naturally gifted when it comes to the power of dance. I met her after the show and we went for a drink at this ace bar before going back to me room to show her me knob. She fought it were beautiful so she gave it a kiss. What a lovely woman.

After the night of spicy black magic in every hole I were bought to an even bigger hole – t' Grand Canyon. We'd arranged a flight in a 'elicopter – or if you're American a 'chopp–or' – to fly us over the grandest of canyons!

You could throw 10 million marshmallows into t' Grand Canyon and it wun't even fill it half way. Unless those marshmallows were as big as the Royal Albert Hall where I once saw Wet Wet Wet. It were absolutely breathtaking. Then I fell asleep. Roy had to nudge me to wake me up. It were proper amazing, but I were sleepy! We'd done a lot of travelling – and filming for this show were 24/7. It were like a reality telly show. There weren't a script so they just had to film everyfing.

They dropped me off in t' middle of t' Grand Canyon and then flew off and left me to get aerial shots of me. There I stood all by meself in t' middle. I fink about it now and all I can fink is I wish I'd had a wank so I could just drop into an interview that the strangest place I'd ever pumped fist were in t' Grand Canyon. That's if that question ever came up. Which it does sometimes. That one, and 'what would ya do if ya were invisible?' I'd go round to Kelly Brooks' house to see what's going down or should I say 'who'.

Our next stop were Montana, passing briefly through Seattle. Ya know that place from the film *Sleepless in Seattle*, starring Tom Banks and Meg Ryan. Dint see either of 'em two there as we were only there for about an hour. Would've been nice to see 'em to see if they were still sleepless.

When we arrived the hotel, it were nofing like the one in Vegas. It were very strange, like a hotel within a hotel, and a bit scary, like somet out of a horror film, *The Shining*, or somet. In the morning we were due to go t' Testicle Festical, where lots of crazy bastards gather to eat

'mountain oysters'. That's what they call them ya know – mountain oysters are bulls bollox. Crazy bastards! It were a proper eye opener I can tell ya!

I fink we must have been the first there that morning. There were a few bikers there, which were a clue as to what kind of people were gonna be there. When I say 'bikers' I mean like proper film-style bikers from 'ell, wearing German helmets with raccoon tails hanging from t' back. I remember finking, 'It's gonna get a bit strange round 'ere', pecifically when we were sat just having a cuppa and a woman walked in wearing a cowboy hat, a bra, biker boots and some black lacy stockings and nowt else. I looked at her minge, then back up at Ben the Director. Then both me and Ben looked at the minge. Don't know how we kept a straight face. I knew this were just gonna be a crazy day.

As the day went off and t' Testicle Festical got busy, we got to see many other ladies' minges. Many of 'em had tattoos of butterflies or eagles down there, which they wanted to show off. And it got odder and odderer. I remember one bloke just walking around drunk, saying 'I've only got one nut' – and he weren't even lying. There were lots of different events going on, girls fighting in oil, horse shit bingo and, of course, the main event ball munching, the winner being the person who consumed the most within an allotted time. Don't know how many times I must of said that on telly. It's always an 'allotted time'.

Of course, I had to taste a testicle meself and it tasted a lot like chicken. A really shite chicken nugget. As it got later, the place got more drunken and wired. It reminded me of that film *From Dusk Till Dawn*, where they all turn into vampires so we fought it best to get

outta there before it got dark and they all started vamping out to try to suck and fuck us.

The little town we stopped at next were a real cowboy town. And the people on the farm that we were staying at were lovely. I really fitted in. Everyone had a tash! I fink cowboys are cool. Even the old fellas look cool. Nice smart jeans, cowboy hat and boots and lovely shirts. One cowboy I really hit it off with were Tim, and that's not just cos I wanted to have it off with his daughter, who were fit as a butcher's dog, I just really hit it off with him. Right nice fella he were, but I dint want to have it off with his daughter and I fink she wanted to have it off with me. I dint have it off with her though out of respect for Tim. But I wanted to. She were Bang Tidy!

I really loved being a cowboy and hanging out on the ranch. It suited me. In this episode, I also did a sketch with Mel C from t' Spice Girls. I'd had a go on both of the Mels. The idea were that I'd got her up the duff and I had to come back from the United States of America cos she cudn't cope. Most of *World Tour* were real, but we had little fings like the Mel C sketch in there just to meke it that more comedically-led. (I fink that's the most serious fing I've ever said...) Anywhere, Mel were great. Brilliant actress. I have banged her, but I'm not the father of her kid and I'm willing to do a DMA test to prove it. She's a lovely lady is Mel. Bunton's another lovely lady, who I've also banged and I'm not the father of her kid either. She's got lovely kids and her fella is a top bloke too. Good for a booze-up!

Mexican midget wrestling

After America we flew to Mexico, which were located on the mouth of the shark. I never knew a country could be so highly and densely populated with old men with wrinkly tomato faces, old women with wrinkly tomato faces and old children with wrinkly tomato faces.

I were a bit nervous about Mexico. Not sure why, because when we got there it were right nice (parts of it, anywhere). We started off in a place called Cancun. It were like a right nice holiday resort really. Not what I expected at all.

There were lots of young funky people partying on t' beach. I hooked up with this bird. She had legs the colour of hot dogs and she were suffering for me! So I gave it to her. Only fair to put her out of her misery. Our tour guide looked like Penfold from *Danger Mouse*. We did a lot of interesting fings in Mexico. I watched Mexican wrestling, and then took part in a wrestling match meself. Not any old wrestling though. No, no, no! I did Mexican midget wrestling .Now, just because the midget I were wrestling were the size of a small boy, it dint mean that he dint have some serious power behind him. I'm not sure why he were being so rough with me, though. We only wanted a demo of a few moves for the camera. Little bastard.

'Ere's a bit of trivia for ya, if ya ever get in a mass debate about Mexican midget wrestling use these facts to dazzle the person ya are conversing with with your knowledge... The wrestlers can never be seen in public without their masks, even if they're having a day off and are playing out with their mates on their BMXs. They sometimes even wear their beautiful decorative masks in t' shower if they don't wanna get their hair wet.

If you're wondering what the PC term is for a 'Mexican midget wrestler' – it's a 'dwarf', 'umpa–lumpa' or a 'monkey man'. Perhaps, there in't a pecific term. They're not bothered what they're called, as long as they're being paid.

Indulging further into Mexican culture we went to a witchcraft market. They sold lots of voodoo trinkets, including voodoo balls, voodoo sheep, voodoo pigs, voodoo beards and voodoo Scooby Doos. Oh, and how could I forget? Voodoo trumpets, of course.

I went to the Mayan city in Mexico as well. It were fascinating. The Mayan city were a restored ruined city that were still a bit ruined, if truth be told, but apparently it'd been restored. It were where they filmed the Mel Gibson film *Apocalypse Now*, which were all about Mayans, I fink. It's a big shame that he got drunk and went all racist, but he's since said sorry so we've gotta forgive him, I guess. After all, he were once Mad Max and he were in *Lethal Weapon* which were ace too. More pecifically *Lethal Weapon 2* with Patsy Kensit. She is one of me favourite MILFs. She's got right blowy lips. Oooosh!

I went into the Mexican jungle, where there were poisonous trees. I got all dangerous and manly like when I saw the trees but when I went to see a bullfight I actually turned into a woman. I fink that were the first

time I've ever cried. It really saddened me when they killed the bull. Poor bastard bull. I swam with dolphins, too, while I were in Mexico, but I'm not such a big fan of the dolphin, I prefer the bulls. Anyfing that laffs that much has an alternative motive. Plus I feel compelled to stick me finger in their blow hole. It's not just a dolphin's hole. Any hole. I always wanna stick me finger in them.

It were a valuable trip, Mexico, and I learned a lot. Apparently Mexicans dint discover shoelaces until 1946, so it's a country that's obviously gone through hardship, but it's still a very lovely place. A word of warning to ya in case ya ever go to Mexico. Too many chillies can wreck ya arse. It must have been the start of me piles cos by the time I got to me next stop, Egypt, me backside were like a scrap yard!

Me at the Mayan City!

Egyptian piles

So, there I were in Egypt, some might say funnily enough situated on the shark's rectum. I'd been there before and wun't right into it. But this time, I had a tour guide with me that should know all t' best bits of Egypt to show me. His name were Rami and he did. He also looked a bit like the guy from *Jurassic Park*.

The first place that Rami took me to were this market. It reminded me of Chapeltown in Leeds. It were full of keyrings in the shape of pyramids and sphincters. Many of the people seemed to have teeth like sugar puffs. I stuck out like a sore finger. And as we were walking through the market, Rami asked me to hold his hand. I were a bit uncomfortable with it at first but apparently it is a sign of manuality in Egypt and nowt to do with hormones.

After the market, we went on a desert safari. Din't see any elephants though. I travelled on a camel but now my behind were in excruciating pain. Don't think the camel ride helped me arse crack, and after having it inspected by a doctor, I realised that I had piles. It killed like no pain I'd ever experienced. Apart from an in-grown toenail. In fact, that's what it felt like, an in-grown toenail in me arse hole.

I remember Roy saying to me, 'welcome to the world of piles! Once ya get them, ya have 'em for the rest of your life'. But, touch wood, I've never had 'em since.

The ones I got, just so happened to be external. I dint know that at the time. Roy told me if ya get piles ya should try to shove 'em back up ya crack. Now, at this time I dint know mine were external, so I were trying to shove 'em up where they'd never been. It were really embarrassing showing the doctor. I knelt on all fours like she were gonna put a strap on and do me doggy-style. She told me to lie down in the foetal position and told me to relax as she were gonna insert her finger. I couldn't relax. I told her if she shoved her finger up me, I'd snap it off with me arse flaps. No chance. She gave me a bit of cream and some suppositories and I were on me way. I remember I recorded the first time I stuck one up me for me video diary for t' show. At first, me arse just wun't accept it. Then, as if it had a mind of its own, it snatched the suppository off me and consumed it quicker than ya could say 'Ooooosh!' The anus is an amazing invention.

Maybe the fact that I were having so much trouble with me bum were, and still is, the reason I have bad memories of Egypt. I remember the morning we were

set to get a hot air balloon ride over the River Nile. It should've been amazing, but I were in amazing pain from the Dreaded Pile. I were in so much pain, I felt drunk. It were madness.

Me celebrity guest that were joining me in me Egyptian adventure were Samia Smith who plays Maria in *Coronation Street*. Yes, that's right, the fittest girl on t' street! Well, equal fittest with Michelle Keegan. I'd love to have a minge tout with those two.

We went on a camel safari together. Oh, the way she mounted the three lipped beast (yes they've got three lips!), it sent a quiver down me private sectors. But I'm not sure I'm a natural camel lover. Horrible creatures. They're like some kind of monster from *Star Wars*. Anywhere, after riding on the humpy bastards for I don't know how long, we settled down on a Bedwinner campsite (Egyptian gypsy camp, basically), where we ate a goat and I serenaded Samia. I sang 'I fink we're alone now' by Tiffany, a ginger pop star of the 80s with big bangers.

I wish we had been alone cos she looked fit, man. And the nice fing about Samia is that she's a lovely down-to-earth girl. Not one of those stuck up bints that knows they're fit. Her fella at the time had come along too. Top bloke! But like I said, I wished we'd been alone, then maybe I could've seduced her with me Lemony love sword.

I'm still in touch with Samia and I'm always running into her at dos and stuff. In fact, saw her only t' other week at the RTS Awards which stands for Royal... actually not sure what it stands for. I dint win, anywhere. I were against the legends of Ant and Dec, so they won.

Nowt against 'em winning anyfing though as they're good lads. I wonder if they'd sell me a couple of their awards...?

Rather than going to the RTS Awards, I could've done with staying in that night cos the next day I had a double recording of *Celebrity Juice*. Not easy filming with a hangover. Nearly as bad as filming with an arse full of piles. Jesus it hurt. I can remember Rami, the tour guide, getting me one of those Egyptian dresses they wear. Had a nice draft going up it to sooth me poorly bum. I also had one of those Tommy Cooper red hats. If it wun't for me fick Northern accent, you'd swear down I were an Egyptian. Dint 'alf look the part.

We had a backflash sketch in this episode, which had me auditioning for *The X Factor*. I'd got to boot camp stage and were at Sharon Osbourne's house. I were singing with me band 'Up North', featuring meself and one of me mates, Jonesy. We sang 'I don't know much' by Aaron Neville. Anywhere, Sharon fought he were good and I were shite so I decided to split up and go solo. I told her that I had a kid that were gonna die when it were a bit older and she still didn't wanna put me through. But Sharon din't really know what she were

Me and me guide

talking about. I knew I could sing because when I was youngerer one of me uncle's was pretty well off and he had a karaoke machine. We use to go round every weekend and have a bit of a sing song and everyone said that I sounded like Simon Le Bon. Anywhere, she might not have fought I had t' X Factor but Sharon's a lovely sexual woman. I bet she knows what she's doing in bed, or stood up in t' kitchen over t' sink or in t' garden behind t' shed.

So, anywhere, where were I? Oh, in Egypt.

What else did I do? I went scubby diving in t' Red Sea but I weren't right into that as when I were about seven I had a bad dream that my tallywhacker had a fish face on t' end of it so I weren't too keen to get in the water with those bastards. That's about it really. So, I'm gonna go now. Ta-ra for a bit.

Hello, I'm back! Just got back from t' hairdresser's for a trip and some highlights. That sounds a bit hormone, dint it?

Just tweeted Rosie a poem to cheer her up. She's hurt her foot. I fink she fell over drunk. Anywhere, I wrote...

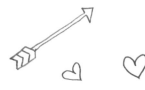

Rosies foot's red
My mind is blue
I miss you so much
Wanna finger blast you X

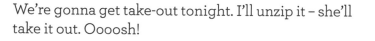

We're gonna get take-out tonight. I'll unzip it – she'll take it out. Oooosh!

Australia, the Land of Priscilla and Neighbours

Well, from Egypt, mostly known for the adventure film *The Mummy* starring Brendon Fraser and *Jewel in t' Nile* starring Michael Douglas, it's onto Australia, known for the film *Priscilla Queen of t' Desert, Neighbours* and *Home and Away*. It's situated near the shark's back foot. Can I just point out that this weren't the order that the episodes appeared on t' telly but the order that we travelled in. That were just a bit of trivia for ya. Ya can use that to impress your mates.

I'd never been to Australia previously so I were very excited. Our first stop were a small town. I can't for the life of me remember what it were called, but it were in the bush district. It were very stereotypical outback Australia. We were staying above a pub. All made of wood in t' middle of nowhere. There were no lock on me bedroom door. But the owners seemed very nice. I remember the first night being woke up by the sound of tap dancers. I went down stair to t' bar area and there were a pissed-up Roy (the camera man) clapping and enjoying what looked like Australia's answer to River Dance. There were a line of blokes tap dancing and Roy were loving it. I told 'em (in a raised voice cos I were a little bit pissed-off cos I'd been woken up) that we had to be up early in t' morning for a local poetry festival fing. We both went to bed. I quizzed Roy about his secret obsession for Ozzy tap dancers. Willy smoker.

Anywhere, the next morning I were a bit nervous about this poetry fing, but nobody knew who I were so I just fought 'Keith! Go and enjoy yaself.'

I had nowt prepared so I just freestyled it. They all fought I were shite, but I weren't shite. I just don't fink they understood me references. As ya can see from me poem to Rosie, I'm actually quite poetically-minded. Anywhere, this were a mad town, but fun and they were having some kind of sporting event in which all the town took part. Like a mini Olympics. So, in t' afternoon, in a bid to regain me dignity, I entered the dunny race, which basically involved a couple of young 'uns dragging a 'dunny' or a toilet on wheels. I lost at that as well.

Finally we went deeper in t' bush all dressed in drag to replicate *Priscilla Queen of t' Desert*. And then we had a flight booked out of there. Ya wun't believe how many flies there were, though. It dint pick up too much on

camera, but there were swarms of them. Weird how they feel so wet when they fly in ya eye. I fink I swallowed a few and all.

The pilot of the plane
that were flying outta
there to our next location were a top bloke
and had hung with us while spending time in that little
town. I purposely befriended him so he'd let me have
a go on his plane. It were only a little plane and we were
a bit worried that it weren't gonna get us up in the air.
I were sweating buckets. It were hot on there. I fought
I were gonna sweat so much I'd be reduced to the size
of Prince.

Flying the plane were a piece of piss in the end. Ya just
had to keep the fingy-majig in t' middle of the watsit.
While I were doing that, the pilot were doing loads of
maths to meke sure we were flying to the right place.
I fink he had the harder job. I'm shite at maths. We
landed in another part of Australia. Again I cudn't
remember where we were. But it were nice little hotel,
this time with locks on t' door.

We'd arranged to go and see a man called the Barefoot
Bushman, who had an old run-down zoo full of
monsters. Crocodiles, Kangaroos and worst of al Koala
bears! They look cute, but they've got retractable razor
sharp claws like little furry Freddie Kruegers, the little
bstards. The Barefoot Bushman were nice enough,
but a bit crazy. But I like crazy people. I fink they're
interesting. He had me sat on a 14, no 16 – well, might
have been 20 to 25 foot-long – croc. I were sweating and

absolutely shitting meself. There were a brown onion farm in me pants. I cudn't honestly remember how he got me to do it. The crew were egging me on and I guess I just fought, 'hey! While I'm 'ere, I may as well'. It's a very manly fing to do sit on a croc. And not many men can say they've sat on a massive croc!

The Bushman took me into what he called the 'Croc's Kitchen' (the pond that it lived in). He spoke about how crocs have bad press – ya know, like sharks have cos of the film *Jaws*. He said they're not really man-eating monsters and that crocs doing death rolls is just in films. A 'death roll' is where they roll around their prey and take 'em to t' bottom to drown 'em before eating 'em. He demonstrated that it were all just a myth using a dummy (which I named 'Nigel'). As soon as he threw Nigel into t' water, what d'ya fink 'appened? The croc death rolled it straight away. See... they're just evil bastards.

After that, we went to Sydney, home to the Sydney Opera house. Architecturally ahead of its time some say, its creamy concrete wings are the sails of the first fleet (see, I know some fings). To me though they looked like loads of chicken beaks. Good though. There were a lot of hot totty in Sydney. I fought I would bump into Kylie or Danni at some point, but I dint. I've since met Kylie and she were a vision of beauty. But back then she were one of the people I'd always wanted to meet and have sex with. She's a proper little spinner, in't she?

As well as the Sydney Opera House, Australia is famed for its many beaches, so quicker than Crocodile Dundee could say 'that in't a knife, this is a knife', I hit one of its many beaches. Lucky for me there were a

group of birds on t' beach who were part of a volleyball team. Cos I'm attractive, they let me join in. I learned how to surfboard while I were there, too. I've never done it since, but I still keep my surfboard propped up in the kitchen. Ya never know when you're gonna be able to drop it into conversation.

I also met up with Paul Robinson (aka Stephan Denis) from *Neighbours*. What a lovely man he is. I expected him to be taller than me, but stood next to me he looked like Frodo from t' *Lord of t' Rings*.

Australia were a lovely place, but I wun't rush back in a hurry – apart from when I'm appearing on ITV2's *I'm a Celebrity Get Me Out of Here!* It takes effing ages to get there. It's like time travel. On a plane for 24 hours? Madness.

Dint bump in t' Kylie once!

Right. Now I'm hungry. Gonna have to meke me a sandwich or somet. Hold on a tick. I'll be two minutes. Unless I've got nowt in t' fridge then I may have to pop out t' shops. It's gone crazy recently. People in t' street say 'hello' and I fink to meself, 'Do I know ya? Have I worked with ya?' Sometimes I'll even end up going for a pint with 'em before I realise I dint actually know 'em at all. It's mental. Can't buy porn from me local shop any more either. Mind, I don't really use porn any more. Got me lovely Rosie to be all dirty with. I remember the good old days when I were a little kid I'd find porn in t' bushes all t' time. Ya never find porn in t' bushes now cos kids dont steal their dads' porn anymore, they just go online, dint they? Wait till their mam and dad have gone to bed, then get on that computer and wank their little eyelashes off.

Right sandwich! Be back in a bit.

How do! I'm back. Had a ham sandwich, some of those salt and vinegar twirl crisps and some apple juice. That's healthy, in't it? Then I gave me right arm some exercise. I were feeling a bit horny. Martine McCutcheon were on t' telly selling good bacteria. Don't know how ya can have good bacteria. Ya can have a good bash when she comes on t' telly though. I don't know what she's up to, Martine McCutcheon, just doing telly ads. I wish she'd get back on t' telly properly in a film. I fought she were great in that film *Love, Actually*. Would love to bang 'er.

Magical Icelander tour

So, nextly and lastly in me Very Brilliant World Tour, I were in Iceland. Not the shop but the country named after it, situated on the shark's back flap, or fin as experts might call it.

Me Iceland tour guide were called Enrick. I expect ya don't spell it like that, but I expect he won't be reading this. If ya are, Enrick, I hope all's well and I've still got me fingers crossed for ya that they do a follow up to *Beauty and the Beast*. He told me that he did the voice for The Beast for the Icelandic version of *Beauty and the Beast*.

What were it he use to say? Oh, I know...

'If ya want me to, I can do it for ya, my lady.'

I would ask, 'do what? What is it ya can do for her, Tom?' (Although he were called 'Enrick' I called him 'Tom' cos he looked like Tom Hanks from *Big*, *Bachelor Party* and *Forrest Gump*. Good film *Forrest Gump*. 'Life were like a box of chocolates. Ya never know what ya gonna get'. Well, that's not 100% true, is it really? It's likely that if you're eating a box of chocolates, ya know what ya gonna be eating is a chocolate. Ya hardly gonna buy a box of chocolates and find a crabstick in there, are ya? And if ya did, I expect you'd take 'em back. But yeah, it's a great film. It'd meke more sense though if he'd said, 'life is like a shopping trolley filled with different food and if ya pick somet out of there

Poor Dermot is terrified of puffins

blindfolded, then ya probably never know what ya gonna get.'

Anywhere, here are some basic facts about Iceland: (If ya know lots of fings ya can impress the ladies by showing them you're much cleverer than them, they love that!) Firstly, the postal service is reliable and efficient and rates are comparable to those in Leeds or other northern cities.

Secondly, to say 'Hello' in Iceland ya say 'Hello'.

First stop to experience true Icelandic fings were a visit to the Blue Lagoon. A manmade lagoon, made by men, the Blue Lagoon is known as the social mecca of Iceland and the pulling rate there is equal to that at the Playboy Mansion. Ya can pull there even if ya like computers. As well as checking out birds and having a little paddle, one of the features there is this troff fing filled with silica mud. People put this on their face like a 'mud mask' sort of fing and it is said to possess magical powers and turn a munter into a Bang Tidy bird. Which is the reason there's lots of fit birds in Iceland that look like models. Apart from Björk. I'm not saying she's a munter, I actually find her attractive. I've always wanted to have a go on her, but she dont look like a model, does she? She's fit though. An't seen or heard from her for a while. When she did that song 'Oh, So Quiet', I liked her. I bet she's crazy in bed. I've always said that one of me good mates Paloma Faith looks like the bastard daughter of Björk and Billie Piper. I'd have it off with all three of 'em at the same time.

I remember when Tom took me to see a geezer. I don't mean a man about a dog but a geofermal hot spring that shoots into t' air. Very exciting! I don't mean that sarcastically either. It were ace! Although I had to film it meself cos me and Roy had a fallout. For some reason, he kept talking while I were doing me opening link about the geezer. Going on and on about the battery on t' camera running out. Don't know why he just dint stop and bang another in. Anywhere, he accused me of being ageist, which is not true at all. It's not me fault he's so old like Yoda and I dint hold it against him. In fact, I pity him that he's so old, he's going daft. Apparently he said he got on t' computer and sent an email to his lawyer. I dint hear owt though. Fing is, I dint fink Roy could use a computer. He's too old. (I love ya really, Roy, if you're reading this. He knows that. Silly old bint.) Anywhere, we made up and we continued on our magical Icelander tour with Tom Banks.

I'm terribly hungover at the moment. It were the *Celebrity Juice* combined with *Lemonaid* wrap party last night, and me back is aching. Fink it's with all t' sex I've been having recently. And cos I'm a bit older. Can't believe I'm gonna be 29 next week. That's me real age – on telly I always say I'm 27 and a 'arf. I fink I can get away with it. Young at heart, young in visual appearance.

Just found out that *Juice* is up for two BAFTAs! The Best Entertainment Programme and the YouTube Audience Award. It's at the end of the month, so I should still be writing this book. I'll let ya know what happens.

I loved Iceland, but it weren't 'arf expensive. Ten quid for a pint! So, we took our own sneaky booze in t' pub with us. I'm not paying ten quid! I use to have a full night out for a tenner when I were a lad, and still have enough left over for a kebab.

After a night of drinking our own sneaky booze in a posh bar full of model-like quality totty, it were the morning and we planned to hook up with the headmaster of the Fairy School. The headmaster came onto me, but the school he were headmaster of weren't hormone sexually related. It were 'Fairy' as in Tinkerbell. In Iceland, a large majority of people believe in the existence of fairies and trolls. Piles of rocks are piled up among the wasteland and it is said that fairies and trolls are responsible for this. Meself, I don't believe in fairies and trolls and there were nowt the headmaster could say or show me to meke me believe otherwise.

At the end of showing me his pictures of said fairies, the headmaster asked whether it were now time we took our clothes off and had a look at each other... I told him it were *not* and were outta there quicker than ya can say '*Sha-ting!*' (For the sake of accuracy, that's actually a word I'd not yet start using yet; that word were born during a rehearsal for *Juice*).

So from fairies, I went sailing in an iceberg water forest, which is what other people call a lake with some big ice cubes in it. Apparently it were used in *Superman 2* featuring Terrence Stamp as General Zod (I fink that were his name). Best baddy ever, General Zod. I can do a wicked impression of him. It doesn't work in writing though so there's no point, but if ya bump into me on t' street or in t' boozer ask me to do it and I will.

The next day, I went to a penis museum. Not that I'm interested in looking at cock, but we fought it might meke for good telly, edgy like. It were full of animal cocks, mostly whales. Some of 'em were terrifying. They looked like weapons. The man who owned the museum were called Mr Ciplin and it's the only tally wacker museum in the world apparently. They dint have one minge in there. Mr Ciplin had a really small cock. It use to belong to a cat. Apparently it's the only cock with a bone in it. And there was one so small you had to have a microscope to see it! Poor bastard.

Of course, Iceland is known for inventing Vikings, as seen in the film *Lord of t' Rings*. I went to a Viking Hotel to learn about the history of them. One of the phrases that they teached me were 'a man is a man and a word is a word'. I confess, I an't got an effing clue what it means, but it sounds good, don't it?

Joining me in Iceland were me pal Dermot O'Leary. He's terrified of puffins. He shared a bed with me, he were that scared. I dint mind cos I don't really like puffins that much meself, and the place where we were staying were surrounded by them. Imagine somebody shoving a puffin in your mouth. Horrible.

We went on a glacier on snowbike fings. That were ace! I stopped for a piss and almost froze me dick off. It were freezing then it got even colderer when we sat down to do an interview. It were ridiculous. There were a snowstorm just as we started the interview. This were back when Dermot had just started *The X Factor* so I wanted to get the lowdown on Cowell. He's a very mysterious character, but me being me, I just came out and said it.

'Tell me somet about Cowell'

I fought Dermot could interpretate that question however he wanted and we'd find somet out. But he dint tell me anyfing of interest really. Very nice like that is Dermot. He ain't a gossip. He's a proper gent...even if he is scared of puffins!

We headed back to the place we were staying at and watched the Northern Lights. Well we dint really. We cudn't see em so they put 'em in t' sky in post-production special FX!

It were great doing *World Tour* and I learnt a lot. I often get asked if I'm gonna do another, but it in't really up to me. It's up to the telly bigwigs.

Anywhere, before the show were released on DVD, I had to do promotion for it on t' telly. Then promote it on DVD. One of me most memorable appearances that I can remember were when I went on *Loose Women*. I've been on a few times since then, but it were me first time and I remember it well. I were a bit nervous. It's weird when the nervous fing happens cos normally I don't give a crap about what people fink of me. But now and again this nervous fing happens. I guess deep down I do care what people fink of me. Maybe that's why I spend three hours in t' hairdresser having highlights done. I'm naturally strawberry blond. I just have it enhanced now and again to meke it betterer. So, anywhere there I were stood backstage and I dint have a clue what I were gonna say.

I rarely plan owt. I just say what I'm finking at time. Then I fought to meself, 'I know! I'll just tell 'em me piles' story. Is that appropriate for daytime telly?'. Turns out it went down a storm. They loved it!

People always fink I'm gonna eff and jeff when I'm on daytime, or they say 'were it 'ard for me to control meself?'. I don't have tourettes though. Yeah, I swear on *Celebrity Juice* cos it's past t' watershed fing, and I've swore in this book a couple of times already, but that's cos I'm a bit childish and I like seeing swearwords written out on t' paper.

Fuck, bugger, tits, arse hole, wank!
See. I use to put swearwords in me SAs at school just to see what the teacher would say.

I never swear in front of me mam though, and cos she watches *Loose Women,* there's no way I were gonna swear on it. So I told 'em about me piles and me trip to the docs, but a daytime edited version like. I demonstrated how the doctor looked at me arse on t' bed, using the *Loose Women* desk as the bed, and I'm talking 'em through it when suddenly I felt the desk go. I broke it! I shit meself and so did Andrea McLean, bless her. She's lovely is Andrea McLean, like Snow White. I bet she's dirty in the sack too. Lisa Maxwell is fit, an' all. Like Emma Bunton's older sister. Not too much older, like.

Talking of which, I were out with Bunton last night. I went to t' Soap Awards and presented the award for Sexiest Female to Michelle Keegan. She is Bang Tidy! She's more classic beauty than sexy though. It's like Jesus laid an egg and out crawled Keegan. She's visually perfect and has a lovely personality to match. So nice and grounded. I'd definitely bash her rat. I met Jacqui Dixon from *Brookside* too. Use to love her when *Brookside* were on. She were always in a shellsuit carrying an oversized handbag coming back from t' swimming baths. Love to take *her* swimming! I tell ya what, she an't changed. She were lovely. If me romance with Rosie weren't blossoming so much I might have got me heels in there with 'er... Yeah, I'd have a go on her, and Keegan and Samia Smith. But, it dint matter as it's going well with Rosie. She gets me, I fink. I flirt and say a lot of shite but she just takes it on t' chin...

I also went on *The Paul O'Grady Show* to promote the *Very Brilliant World Tour*. I use to love that show when it were on. Haven't seen O'Grady on t' telly for a while. I fink he's brilliant and a right nice man. It's so strange when ya meet these people that ya right like and it turns out they like what ya do, too. So, yeah, I went on there and I'd just come back from me holiday and had an eye infection. I looked like Rocky (hero!). It'd proper swelled up. Looked like I had a twat growing on me eye so I figured if jizum can meke humans, surely it can cure me swollen eye. So I pumped fist and put a bit of me man milk on me eye, and d'ya know what? It cured it. I told Paul O'Grady I were gonna bottle it up and sell it to Boots. Who'd have fought me jizum had magical healing powers? I mention all of this on t' show, but just editing out certain words so I could get away with it

on daytime telly, while also saying *Keith Lemon's Very Brilliant World Tour* on ITV2 10pm a lot. *Cha'mone motha plugga!* I pride meself on me pluggin skills. I've got no shame when it comes to promoting fings. When I've made somet I'm proud of, I wanna tell everyone about it. Been that way since I were a young 'un. If I'd had a right good perfect poo, I'd shout me mam and say 'Come 'ave a look at this pipe I've laid!'.

Drinks like a tramp

Moving t' big smoke

When *The Very Brilliant World Tour* came out on DVD, I were off again this time on a small regional promotional tour, going to local radio stations and stuff and doing a bit more TV and signings. I went on Channel 5's *Studio Five Live*, I fink it were called. Did that a few times. Matthew Wright were a nice bloke – *not* Matthew Wright, I mean *Ian* Wright. Matthew Wright is a nice bloke, though. I like him on t' *Wright Stuff*. I'd like to do a show like that. Or like Jeremy Kyle. I fink I'm good with people. I watch that Jeremy Kyle and I fink one day one of those loonies is gonna crack him.

I did a photoshoot in *Heat* magazine with me mate, Olivia Lee. That were fun. Olivia is as funny as she is fit. I fink it's rare for someone to be that funny and fit, cos in the back of t' mind their fitness distracts from their funniness. But Olivia always seems to pull it off.

Anywhere, then I went on a signing tour up and down t' country. I went back to Leeds and did a signing in HMV. I weren't sure if anyone would turn up, but they did and they were all right nice. A few birds there that I would've finger blasted too! Still fink it's odd when someone asks ya to sign a lemon. What are they gonna do with it? Good when they ask ya to sign their bangers though. When they ask me to do that I get a right good hold and spend some time on it. I draw a self-portrait and put 'Keith woz 'ere', with an arrow pointing down t' tit slit. At this point in me life I decided that if I were gonna meke a go of it on t' telly as a TV host or an entertainer or whatever it is I were, I fought it best to move to London. It were a big step but I knew a few people there. I weren't seeing Rosie back then. We'd got off with each other now and again, but she weren't me bird yet so it weren't like I were leaving her behind.

It's good Signing bangers

Keith woz ere!

Me mam encouraged me to go live me dream. She were always behind what I did apart from when I were a kid and I got done by the police for filling a school toilet with stones through a skylight window. Got bolloxed then.

So, I left Leeds to live in t' Big Smoke. I got a right nice place in the centre of town and even MTV's *Cribs* wanted to come and see it! Madness. I were a bit dubious about doing *Cribs*. It's a bit showy offy in't it? I heard someone once did *Cribs* and two weeks later they got robbed. Not sure if that's true but it is a word of warning. But in the end it were good to do, it felt a bit like I'd arrived. In a small way. Not like those American *Cribs* ya see with their big fuck-off houses... Me place were nowt like that. In fact none of the English *Cribs* are like the Americans. Caprice's *Cribs* were good though! Don't know if ya saw it. In her basement, she had a dance floor. Apparently she did a bit of DJing on t' side. Somet I've been asked to do but I always say no cos I'm not a DJ. I tell a lie. I did it for a *Heat* magazine party once. That's only cos Lucy Cave asked me. I like 'er. She's got hair like me. In fact if she had a tash she'd look like me, apart from she has a bangers and gash. Anywhere in Caprice's dance floor, she had a massive disco ball, too. The floor were lowered into the ground and water came in turning the dance floor into a pool. She must've made some money to afford a gaff like that. It were truly amazing.

Obviously I've got a right nice gaff too, I just an't got a dance floor that turns into a pool. I fought about having a pool put in t' garden, but it's the up keep.

And the British weather is shite, in't it? I wonder how much I'd actually use a pool. I got a treadmill. Used it for six weeks every day, then never touched it again. Boring as fuck is fitness. Ya wun't know it to look at me, but I've never been to a gym in me life. Just three hours of swingball a day.

So yeah, moving to London were exciting, although there were a bit of a language barrier with me accent. For some reason nobody could understand me when I tried to order a glass of coke. I can remember going to a pub and saying 'can I have a glass of coke, please?' and the barman said 'erm, sorry?' and he looked at me like I'd asked him to put his ass on me coke. So I repeated myself, 'can I have a glass of coke?'. Again he said, 'what did you say?' and I fought, 'what does he fink im saying? It don't sound like I'm asking for a bottle of Newquay Brown, 'can I have a bottle of Newquay Brown...' Then I heard someone say, 'can I have a glass of cewk?' and even to this day if you're in t' pub with me, you'll hear me voice change. Ya know how people have a telephone manner, I have an ordering a glass of coke manner.

Anywhere, enough of that! I had a little break before me next telly project. Not by choice, it were just coming up. Sexually everyfing were coming up. I kept myself busy in the meantime – there were plenty of fings to distract me. There were loads more birds in London than in Leeds. I'd already scored with most of 'em in Leeds. I went back to LA on holiday where I stayed at Avid Merrion's hotel again. He were still a crank and had become obsessed with her out of *Charmed*... ya know, Shannon Doherty. He spent most of his time outside her house asking her to spit in his face. Weirdo. Don't fink his wife were too happy about it. She's also his sister. All very strange.

The Spice Girls had also just got back together and were doing a tour so I popped along for a few of 'em. By 'eck they are all FAF. I were right proud of me mate Bunton. It were nice to see her on stage holding a mic instead of a pint of lager for a change. Boy she can drink. The after party were nuts – just Spicy Girls everywhere. Fink Geri fancied me, I could see it in her eyes. I fink we had a strawberry blond connection. Emma introduced me to Victoria and David. I fink she fought I'd be more excited. I'm not right into football, me though. I saw a charity match with Page 3 Girls once and that were amazing. I had a stiffy so long it ached. Cun't wait to get home and bash it off. Victoria were right nice though and she's very funny. David were a top bloke, too. Very polite. One night after the show we went back to Mel B's. She had a lovely gaff – could have been on *Cribs* too! Fink she were quite proud and chuffed to show us round. This right normal Leeds lass from Leeds had done so well. I can remember Mel B from years ago when she use to be a dancer in a place in Leeds called Yell Bar. She were just as fit back then as she is now. One of me mates actually worked with her in a jeans shop as well. I won't go into any of the stories that she told me about Mel cos she might get arrested and I'd hate this to be one of those controversial books like that Ulrika book years ago. I actually saw her a few weeks ago, she were right nice.

Introducing Celebrity Juice

Then one night full of fate, I were out with me mate Kate Thornton celebrating her birthday. I went out with Kate for a bit, but nowt came of it. We went bowling once. I remember her bending down and seeing her fong pop out of her trousers, looked like t' Yorkshire Television logo popping out of her pants, nice. She's fit Kate Thornton. I always fought she looks a bit like Billie Piper, which means she must also look a bit like Paloma Faith and Bjork. Each one of 'em has got the essence of each other in 'em, d'ya know what I mean? I knew ya would. Anywhere, as I were saying it were a fateful night as it were where I met Dan Baldwin, executive producer of *Celebrity Juice*!

It's like Yorkshire television

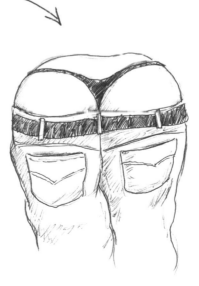

Dan introduced himself to me and said that'd he'd like to work with me, and would I be interested in doing a show with Fearne Cotton and Holly Willoughbooby, who just so happened to be his wife, and still is. He's done well there cos he's not a hunky bloke like me, but he's a good lad and knows his shite. Obviously, I'd already met Holly when I did me *World Tour* and she were lovely. I dint know Fearne. I only knew what I'd seen on telly and I liked her on t' telly. She were proper. Now that I've worked with 'er I can only tell ya that she's the most professional person I've ever met. The most professional person with the most professional nostrils. Her and Holly both, they're brilliant. I would never have fought about working with 'em but I guess that is the genius of Dan putting us all together.

He gave me a treatment for the idea. That normally consists of a piece of paper with what the idea is on it and a cover sheet. Producers like to have a name for the show lined up before they take it to a channel and beg for a commission. Funny fing were I'd just written an idea for a panel show meself called *Keith Lemon's Big Heads*. But I really liked Dan and his idea of *Celebrity Juice* so I gave him me treatment and they took a couple of fings from it and included them in the *Juice* show. I had the late Amy Winehouse in there with different categories for games in her beehive. That went in the first episode I recall.

I tell ya what, I've just been watching *Britain's Got Talent*. Fuckin 'ell, Alesha Dixon is fit. I've met her before like and I always fought she were the fittest when she were in Mystique. But she's just getting fitterer!

It's like magic. If I weren't with Rosie, she'd get it. Can't believe she's never been on *Juice* - or Martine McCutcheon. If you're reading this Alesha or Martine, ya should come on t' show!

Before we actually started the show I went to the V Festival with Holly - not sure what the 'V' stands for. I fink that were a great bonding weekend. Somehow Holly had blagged a Winnebagel. It had a toilet in it, which were a big bonus. I remember seeing a shit pyramid in a toilet at Glastonbury once. I can still see it when I blink me eyes. So Holly says we can only use the toilet for weeing and no solids. If we needed a shit we had to go use the civilian toilets with the civilians. But I remember hearing her in t' toilet. She sounded like an old tramp. Sounded like she were having a fight with her arse and then there were a big fallout. I fought the Winnebagel were gonna tip over. Then she came out with her little angelic face. Face of an angel, arse of a tramp.

I had a great time that weekend. It were exciting to talk about the new show that we were gonna be doing together. I remember while we were drunk, saying it's gonna be good this show, and saying 'I fink it's gonna be big'. Then I told Holly that it is common for most women to have one breast biggerer than t' other and normally it's the left one. I asked her if I could check and she said 'no'. Still, it were a great weekend.

The first time I met Fearne I remember finking she seemed like she were up for a bit of fun and I did fink she had incredibly large nostrils. I fink she is actually a mix of Madonna and Beyoncé. If ya merged them two together, take two photographs and get a computer wizard to put them together and you'll see, it looks like Fearne.

So we started out doing *Juice* in the basement of the TalkBack offices. Fink we did it about three times, once with just a basic camcorder filming it. The guests were different back then too. There'd be a journalist from a tabloid or celebrity magazine a Richard Bacon-type person (who's a good lad and been on *Juice* a few times). I fink Jodie Marsh were on the panel. She's a lovely lass and meke what ya will about her with her new Bruce Lee muscles , when ya see her in person it's quite impressive. She fancies me, but there's never been a window there for me to smash her back doors in. Either she's always been seeing someone or I have. But I'll always be here if she wants some TLC. She's got shit loads of tattoos now, more than Fearne. Fink Fearne's got about 16. They say having tats are addictive, once ya have one ya want another. Bit like wanking, I suppose.

So I fink TalkBack sent a copy of what we filmed in the basement to ITV and they liked it. The people at ITV liked what we filmed! Peter Fincham (The Boss of ITV) and the poshest man I've ever met came to watch us do it live and he liked it! The chemistry between the three of us were there. Both Holly and Fearne were already hooked up with fellas, but they were still giving me the eye. Holly still can't stop touching me and I can see Fearne's nostrils flare with excitement when she sees me, but it weren't the onscreen chemistry we see now. I fink the three of us went to an awards ceremony, fink it were Vodafone, and that were the first time we all got a bit drunk. I can remember pushing it with both of 'em to

Bruce Lee
Muscles

Jodie
Marsh

see where the line were. Fearne had her mouth sucking on me balls whilst Holly stroked and kissed me penis. Just joking... They're both really good sports, with great senses of humour and I get away with murder. Fink that were the first night I mentioned Fearne's massive nostrils. She din t' teck any offence. If I wink at her though she hates it. I fink it's cos it turns her on and she's finding it increasingly hard to fight her emotions for me.

Right, I fink its dinner time. Gonna have a breck. It's me birthday tomorrow so I'll report back to ya what happens and hopefully remember to take some pictures.

Oh my god! It is now the day after me birthday. I am fucked! Just got home from some meetings and put me leopard print PJ bottoms on. Feel mashed up. I had a great day and night though. Went to me fave restaurant in Camden, which is right posh and food is amazing. Ya get a lot of FAF totty in there too. Most of 'em were sat with me: Holly and Fearne, Bunton, Kate Thornton, Cleo Rocos and me boymates. Got a great set of mates in London now. Would've been nice to have some of me Leeds massive down though.

So it were 2008, I fink. We were about to start the first ever *Celebrity Juice*. There weren't too much in the way of a script – 'Sha-ting', 'po-ta-to' and lots of the fings that people fink are catchphrases of the show, they all pretty much happened organically. I fink that's the right word. Sounds good anywhere.

The first show featured Dermot O'Leary (top lad, but scared of puffins as ya know!) Laurence Llewelyn Bowling, a tabloid journalist and me good mate Paddy McGuinness!

In the first episode, I'm not sure Laurence knew how to take me. I don't fink he'd met a Northern person before. I fink he were a bit disgusted with me. He should come on now, it's ruderer than ever. Last time I saw him he were lovely, though. I've always admired his wicked hair. I said 'wicked' as in 'right good' to one of me mates in Leeds and he looked shocked. Fink he fought I'd caught London. I don't fink I'm ever gonna catch London though. I'm Leeds right through to the arse hole.

I remember me outfit as if it were yesterday. I had on a beautiful silver suit what I bought from a shop on Oxford Street called French Eye. Not sure what that name means. Top Man is obvious, it means if ya shop there you'll look like a 'Top Man', and when I do shop there I look like a 'Top Man'. But I also look top when I shop at Zara or H&M or River Island. Not sure what their names are supposed to suggest. But I had this silver suit on and I honestly felt like a million pounds. Before the series I were given a clothing allowance. I cudn't believe it. I just went on a shopping spree buying clobber. I felt like I'd won a competition.

People ask me if I watch *Juice* go out on t' telly when it's on and the answer is if I'm in, I watch just to see what mekes the cut. It's so strange to watch back old episodes. Not that I normally do. When they released the *Celebrity Juice* DVD I watched it again when I did the commentary fingy. The show were a lot tamer back then. I fink I only swore once. I can remember Fearne giving me some jip so I said to her:

'D'ya know what that "F" stands for on t' front of ya desk?'

She said 'What?'

I said, 'Fuckin shut up!'

Ya should've seen the shock on Holly's face. Everyone's face, in fact. It were like I'd punched a baby in t' face. The rest of the series were a lot cleaner back then, but still now and again I'd drop an 'F' bomb 'ere and there. I never set out to be nasty with Fearne, not nasty, just winding her up like. It just happened like that naturally. None of it were planned. Same with Holly, calling her 'Holly Willoughbooby'. It were all a natural process. Her name is Holly and she's got massive boobies. Even her mum calls her Holly Willoughbooby now! Ya can see that we're all really enjoying ourselves. Holly often says that it's her 'night out'. That's what happens when ya have kids I suppose. Holly, she drinks like a tramp. She comes in t' studio with a bottle in a brown paper bag. But I really like it when she says that. Although I dint like it when Fearne started with all that ginger shite. The first time she said it I fought to meself 'Are ya blind? Me hair is the same colour as yours, ya dingbat!' Bigging up Julie from me hairdressers that mekes me hair look so good and strawberry blond!

I fink the first show got around 360 thousand viewers, which apparently were a respectable start. But if we got that now I fink they'd chuck us of air. It's crazy how it's grown.

I don't fink Jedward joined the show until Series 3. Of course back then we had no idea we'd get to Series 2. We were proper chuffed that ITV2 went with it and let it grow. But before I talk about Jedward, who to me are such an integral part of the show, here's a brief run down of some of the people that have been memorable on *Juice*, if I can remember 'em.

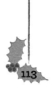

113

The Juice hall of fame

Rufus Hound

Rufus is a lovely man that were so lovely he became a regular panelist. It were great to have Rufus on t' show, nice to have another bloke on to talk about tits and minge. Rufus loved prostitutes and would often wanna go out and pay to smash back doors in. I'm kidding ya dingbats! The whole prostitute fing with Rufus came about when we'd been out for some award fing or other and a prostitute came up to him and asked him if he wanted business. When he said to her it weren't really his fing, she said that she knew some boys that'd suck him off. I were in the taxi about to go home while this were happening so I just saw him talking to the lady of the night, and I've ruined him ever since. To be honest I'm not even sure if it's ever been in the show me talking about Rufus and his prostitute addiction. Anywhere, Rufus is always a good sport. I remember in one show me and Rufus actually snogged. I fink we were playing 'Get ya coat, you've pulled.' It's almost like a game of 'Chicken'. He went to kiss me I fink and I just fought: 'Fuck it. Ya cun't mock it till you've tried it.' It were horrible, but I fink it helped Rufus overcome his curiosity. Rufus has taken his top off a couple of times in the show, too. He's got incredibly big nips and colourful tattoos that match his colourful underpantage.

Jedward

The first time I met Jedward were the weirdest day of me life. All they kept on going on about were 'let's go to Tescos, there's a Tescos near here. Let's go to Tescos, it would be really cool to go to Tescos'. So I asked 'Why would it be cool?' and they said 'I don't know it just would be really cool.' Weird.

On the way back home on the fun bus, no one were speaking and I just piped up and said 'Were that weird or what?' And that got everyone talking. I'm not saying I dint like them but it were weird. But now, I know them right well and I love those boys. At Christmas they phoned me a couple of times going 'Hello Keith, it's Christmas, yayy!' at whatever effing o'clock. 'Santa has come, get up! There's a whole world out there! Let's go get it Keith, let's do this'. But I do love them. I'm sometimes envious of them because they're so close. Imagine ya don't give a shite what anyone finks of ya because your brother, who's just like ya, loves ya so much. I'd bum him I would, and is it a bad fing to bum yourself? If ya could clone yourself, would ya get off with yourself? I would. Just to see what I'm like.

I fink I'm a bit of a mentor to them, I'm like their older brother. They don't drink, they've never had a drink. I want to take them out t' Rhino, get them pissed and get them a lap dance. I'd love to do that, it would break them in to manhood.

The Hoff

The Hoff dint know who I were so I fink he fought I were a bit crazy to begin with, same as Kelly Brook when she first met me – she looked at me like I were a murderer. But he kept trying to copy my accent which I took as a compliment. And now we're proper mates. He's a bit like Jedward in the respect that he don't care too much.

I fink he enjoys being 'The Hoff' and the memory of what's been and gone, but I'm more obsessed with his *Knight Rider* years. I fink he likes to be remembered as Michael Knight, and who wouldn't? Black leather jacket, red shirt... I remember when we filmed with him the second time and we asked what he were wearing and it were a black leather jacket, a red shirt and jeans like Knight Rider and I said cool and turned up with the same gear on.

DON'T HASSLE THE HOFF

Emma Bunton

It is always good having Bunton on t' show. Whenever anyone asks me who the best guest is we've 'ad on I always say anyone who is a mate in real life is best. When you've got someone on that ya know ya can take it further, ya know where that line is and, often with mates there is no line cos they know yer just joking. Emma's lovely and has a great sense of humour and lovely bangers. She's been on so many times now she can more or less deputy captain. If Fearne or Holly aren't on for some reason, I always want Emma there. She's very much like Holly, in fact. Really pretty 'girl next door' but with a dirty mind. I'd love to have a Spice Girls' Special one week. Mel C's been on and she's really nice. So down to earth and Mel B's been on a few times. Mel B always acts shocked by some of the naughtier fings I say, but she's one of the naughtiest women I've ever met. She loves talking about sex. She once asked me if I liked chocolate star-fish. I still don't know what that means.

Eamonn Holmes

He's a lovely warm, funny man. Eamonn has been on *Celebrity Juice* a couple of times. I fink he enjoys himself. He laffs a lot and has a good sense of humour. He's from Belfast and I can talk Belfastian 'Situation'. It's funny with Eamonn cos when I appear on *This Morning*, he mekes out that he don't like me, like that's our on screen chemistry. But he does like me really, I can tell. I fink me and Eamonn should have a night out at Spearmint Rhino.

Claudia Winkleman

I've known Winkletoes a while, although I an't seen her recently. She is so funny, and sexy. I fink she were the first person I ever said 'I would destroy ya' to.

Eamonn likes me really

Saying that were quite shocking back then. I'm not sure the channel knew what it meant cos they used it in a promo that went out pre-watershed. Obviously 'I would destroy ya' is a sexual reference. It's basically saying 'I would sex ya up so vigorous, ya won't be able to walk for a week.' Passionate loving, like. Yeah, she's really cool is Claudia. Got good hair, too.

Paloma Faith

Paloma is brilliant. Right good singer and very creative. Some people confuse that creativeness with craziness. But she an't crazy. People fink I'm crazy, but I'm not. I just like enjoying meself and just like Paloma I sometimes don't have an edit button. Paloma just says what she finks and that mekes for a great guest on a panel show. I fink the first show she were on were with

Tamzin Outhwaite and Bunton. They were all pissed up! It were brilliant. Paloma had a fruit bowl hat on. I had me own, which the props department had made that squirted water from a banana. It had plums at the bottom of the banana to represent bollocks. Obviously the banana were the cock. Yeah, she's great, Paloma. The next time she came on she were slightly quieterer. Fink she'd not drunk as much. She told me she's not really a drinker, a glass of wine and ya can smash her back doors in. I did a charity fing with her once. Me and her hosted it and she'd got loads of music acts involved. It were a great night. Ricky from t' Kaiser Chiefs were there. He's a nice bloke from Leeds! Apparently he bought me a drink once when I loved in Leeds, but I can't remember. Don't worry, Ricky! I'll buy ya one back.

Joe Swash

A right nice ginger lovable dingbat. He says no wrong about anyone, Joe. Top bloke, good for a night out, even though he's so cockney I can't tell what he's saying sometimes. Talks about bouncer balls a lot. Saw him at the Soap Awards t' other night. He were hosting the after party show for ITV2. He had similar light-coloured trousers on like meself. I don't fink he shuck his willy enough after he had a wee. He had a little crop circle. That'll teach him!

Verne Troyer

I class Verne as another good mate. He's in me film, which I'll talk about when we get to that bit. One of the smallest fellas I've ever met, too. I fink woman just wanna breastfeed him and he's always hungry for the tit. A great sport too. I hope to work more with Verne. I'm finking of writing *Gremlins: The Musical,* he'd be great as Gizmo. I actually did a pilot with him, but nowt happened. Not a *Gremlins* pilot but more like a late-night chatshow fing. Maybe we'll rework it though. He just sent me a copy of his *Playboy* issue. *He* were in *Playboy.* Funny, as he's dressed as Hugh Hefner, surrounded by naked women. He's just at the right height for some good old motting out! Oooooosh! I fink one of the most memorable bits of *Juice* were me chasing Verne like a T-Rex. We were acting out scenes from famous films and the panels had to guess what the film were. I know it were one of Fearne's favourite bits. It were nice to see her laffing, miserable cow. Joking, if ya reading this Fearne. Although she probably in't. She's probably too busy painting her bedroom black or somet morbid like that.

Paddy McGuinness

A very good mate of mine, who later became me dancing partner in *Let's Dance for Comic Relief*. Love having Paddy on the show. He's so funny and we have a similar sense of humour. He's a proper man's man. If he weren't married up with an incredibly Bang Tidy wife, I fink Paddy would be me pulling partner when he comes down London. If I weren't with Rosie, of course. I don't go out on t' pull now – just have a little flirt now and again. I'm a bit cheeky but I'm not a love rat!

Dermot O'Leary

Another top lad! Fink he'll be married up by t' time this book is out. So congrats to him. Shit me! Everyone is getting married up. It's great having people like Dermot on t' show cos ya get to see the real them rather than what ya see when they're doing their own shows what they are known for. It's a kinda release as they can do and say what they want and that's me job – to bring that side of 'em out. Of course everyfing is all done in jest. There's no better hug than a hug from Dermot O'Leary... apart from a Kelly Brook hug or a Davina McCall hug. Or a Pamela Anderson hug. Or a Cheryl Cole hug, I mean a Cheryl Tweedy hug, or let's just say a Cheryl hug. Saying that, I don't fink I've had a hug from Cheryl. Have I? Of course, in me dreams I've done all sorts of fings with 'er. Once I had 'er sat on top of me while Kimberly from Girls Aloud were sat on me face. One of the best dreams I've ever had, I fink, pecifically as Sarah and Nicola were lezzing off with each other. Great when ya have those sort of dreams.

man's man

Margret

Janet Street Porter aka 'Margret'

First of all, what a fantastic name! Although for some reason, I always wanna call her 'Margret' or 'Aunty Margret'. I love Margret. She's so opinionated and funny. Easy to wind up, but she plays on it sometimes. A great woman. Apparently Janet likes 'rambling', which is what she calls going for a walk, but in me book it's going 'ra, ra, ra, ra, ra, ra', which is what she does a lot on *Loose Women*. I wonder if she can piss standing up. I bet all those Loose Women can piss standing up! Denise Welsh can for sure. She's a great woman. After she were on *Juice* she flashed me her bangers. I knew she were gonna get 'em out when she were on *Big Brother*. Chuffed she won that. She's a right good egg is Denise. Sexy too! I bet there in't owt she wun't do. Good lass!

I'm just gonna have somet to eat. I'm starving me cock off. I might bash one out as well. Let's just see if Rosie has tweeted me.

Rosie Parker @lemontwittor soon soon soon! Long as I get you to meself soon. You spend more time with Cotton than with me at the moment!

Ooooh, see she finks there's somet going on between me and Fearne. I like that she's a bit jealous. Nice that. Now dinner...

Well, that dish weren't that exciting, but it were healthy. Me healthy oriental meal, as featured in me workout DVD, a lot later on from t' period that we're in now.

But if ya want the recipe 'ere it is:

UNCLE BEN'S RICE!

Bang it in t' microwave for two minutes.

While that's cooking chop up some white cabbage and add some red peppers if ya feeling posh.

Empty a tin of tuner fish on top of that.

When ya rice is done mix it up with the tuner, peppers and white cabbage.

Then add some zing with soya sauce for a healthy taste of the Orient!

Ooooosh...

Anywhere, where was I?

Memorable guests that I can remember. Of course how could I not remember Louie Spence...

Louie Spence

He's such a funny guy. He were a dancer for t' Spice Girls back in t' day. So that programme *Pineapple Studios*, that show had started getting really popular. One week Louie were in t' big magazine we have when we do the cover story round. Most of the people in t' magazine are people that aren't doing as well as they once were, or are meking a comeback, or are just coming up. Well, one week Louie's in there but the next week he were doing so well that he were on the panel, doing the splits and spitting and doing all his Louie Spence-isms. Louie's got a potty mouth so fits right in with the *Juice* gang.

Louis Walsh

From one Louie to another, but this time spelt a bit different. Louis Walsh has been on a couple of times. I love 'R' Walsh, he gossips more than me! I remember the second time he were on he were saying, 'I've got all your DVDs.' I only had one out back then. Then he said 'I don't know what I'm doing. What's this show again?' I said, 'It's *Celebrity Juice*, remember the last time you were on? Well it's that.' I fink when Louis came on it were the first time I said, 'Po-ta-to!' He gave me the phone to Jedward's mam and I just ended up saying everyfing I could fink of that had an Irish link. *'River Dance, U2, Christine Bleakley, Graham Norton, Commitments, PO-TA-TO!'* And it seemed to stick. Every week after, I felt obligated to saying, 'Po-ta-to!' I still get it all the time now if I dint say it in the show they ask, 'WHY?' But I cudn't say it if there's no context – d'ya know what I mean? It's mad when I'm actually buying potatoes in t' supermarket and ya get a chorus of 'Po-ta-to!' from folk. It sometimes feels like a bunch of turkeys following ya. 'Potato, potato, potato!' Or owls.

Peaches Geldof

I remember when we had Peaches Geldof fill in for Fearne while she were away doing one of her many charity fings. Fearne would eat dogshit if it were for charity, she's so good like that. She won't suck me off for charity which is a shame, but I really got on with Peaches. I fought she might have been a bit awkward, but she were right nice and very flirty. Fink she'd've right liked some of me Lemon Juice.

129

Caroline Flack

I always enjoy it when Caroline 'Tiny Hands' Flack is on *Juice*. I'm quite built but ya cock must look massive in her little hands. I know Caroline right well. She's a lovely little spinner. I've got a bit of a festival history with 'er. She's a right goer, festival goer. I knew it were gonna be a little awkward when she came on the show after she'd been doing whatever she'd been doing with that young lad from One Erection, err, I mean 'Direction'. When t' audience are there I cudn't help but sometimes be a little bit naughty and just ask the question that everyone wants to know. Anywhere,

CAROLINE 'TINY HANDS' FLACK

there's an age gap between me and Rosie so I'm not one to talk... except Rosie can buy fireworks and rent *Nightmare on Elm Street* from Blockbuster. Well, he should be able to now, shun't he? Fink he's 18 now. Age in't nofing but a numerical figure. Love is a very powerful fing. Look at *Dracula*. She were about 24 when he were 400! It's none of our business who Flack's banging.

Davina McCall

Lovely Davina has been on *Juice* a couple of times and she's great. A great inspiration who I'd also like to have full penatratitititive sex with her one day. Nofing dirty just to say fanks for all t' support she's giving me. With televisual advice and direction and given me an erection watching her workout DVDs. I have nowt but professional admiration for that sexy goddess and her big French nose. When she were first on *Juice* I remember wearing a white suit that had Velcro down the side so I could rip it of and reveal me gymtastic outfit so she could teach me some moves for when I'd finally release a fitness DVD. She got right stuck in and I eventually ended up simulating a good back scuttling with her. She's such a good sport. I love her.

Matt Horne

Matt Horne were a lovely guest and he taught me how to rave, then I gave him a lesson in Russian Kossack (how the fuck d'ya spell that?) dancing, which is me signature move.

Barbara Windsor aka 'Babs'

Always remember Christopher Biggins passing me on to the phone to Barbara Windsor. I fink ya could see I were a bit startled and starry-eyed about it. Love Babs. She told me I were a bit naughty, which I liked, and she said that *Juice were* a bit like *Carry On*. I were chuffed as I loved the *Carry On* films. I hope *Keith Lemon: The Film* follows in the footsteps of the *Carry On* films. That's what I've tried to create as such. Let's see how it goes. I remember asking Barbara if her bangers still made the honk noise they use to meke in t' films. She said that they did. I were thrilled. It were one of me Leeds massive that first did that noise. I remember 'em saying, "Ere Keith can ya do this noise? *HONK*!' I said, 'I dint know. I'll have ago. '*HONK*!' — and I've been doing it ever since.

Chipmunk

Chipmunk were a good lad, although I fink he were a bit shocked by some of the behaviour. Especially me and Rufus snogging. The look on his face looked like he'd just seen a murder. He were a great sport when we changed his voice into the voice of an actual chipmunk though. Good on 'im. It's good when guys like Chipmunk, Tinchy or N-Dubz loose their street bravado and just become... well, less 'street' for a moment. It's nice to see that side of 'em. Instead of arms crossed, word to ya mam style all 't time.

Philip Schofield aka 'Uncle Phil'

He's another one that drops his street raga-muffin bravado when he's on *Juice* and we get to see the real Philip, whose hair is silver but pubes are as black as a raven's wing, so he told me. We had a great time with Philip. He's been on twice and the second time he were on I fink it were our highest rating episode, just beating the Ant n' Dec one. You've still got it Phil! Never left ya! Oooosh! The second time he came on he told a story about a guest (who I said I wouldn't name) who showed him and Holly her flange all t' way through t' interview. Classic!

Gino D'Acampo

Not sure how many times me mate Gino's been on, but he's lovely and everyone loves him. Of course I always joke that he's in character and that he's actually from Sheffield, but it's not a joke really. He is actually from Sheffield. He does a great Italian accent though, sounds proper. And cos the women love all that Italian stuff he gets away with saying stuff to women that normal fellas can't say. Like the time he said to Fearne with nostrils like she has, 'I bet she can suck like fuck'. I could get away with it, but again I an't normal – I'm just a bit betterer-looking than normal. Gino's a good-looking fella too, so that helps him get away with stuff too. I loved it when Gino and Uncle Phil were discussing Twittor and Gino were saying he weren't gonna follow somebody who had a picture of a bird for their profile picture. 'I'm not gonna follow a bird! Why am I gonna follow an effing bird?' I pissed meself. His theory that if they dint have picture of 'emselves then they have to be ugly. Chris Moyles and Comedy Dave were on that episode too.

GINO FROM
SHEFFIELD

Michelle Keegan

One of me all time favorite sports has gotta be Keegan though. Lovely Michelle Keegan. We've had her limbo-ing, she drank a pint of lager that had jizim in it. She's great fun.

Chris Moyles

Chris Moyles is a Leeds lad. Big up! Just been on t' Chris Moyles' Show today actually. Had a great time. Had a good laff playing 'Guess the TV Theme Tune'. There were a couple I dint get but I'm pretty good at that sort of stuff. Cun't believe I dint guess *Take Me Out*? though. Got *Benson*, *Knight Rider* and *Airwolf* straight away! He an't 'arf lost some timber, Mr Moyles. Not sure how he's been doing it, but good on him. He seems a lot happier. Not that he weren't happy before, but ya can hear it in his voice on t' radio. He just seems happier! Well done, mate! When you've finished with this getting fin stuff let's go for some jars and a kebab.

George Lamb aka 'Lady Killer'

Lady Killer (not that he's actually killed a woman but ya know what I mean). George Lamb were a good sport when he came on and played *Silence of the Lamb*. I had to get a reaction out of him using different methods of getting a reaction in a series of different rounds. For example, 'A Joke', pulling a funny face, doing a dance, insults, or anyfing goes.

...and then the soap stars

Most soap stars are great fun. Jack P. Shepherd is a good lad. He plays that right cocky little bastard in *Corrie*, but he's actually right nice! Antony Cotton is lovely too, as is Kim 'Fit as Fuck' Marsh. Dave Berry has been on so many times we did a montage of his best bits. I fink when Dave were on it were the first time me willy ever popped out while I were doing some sort of strip. I get a lot of people ask me if it really were me willy that popped out. Even me mam phoned me and asked me. Well, I'm not telling. It's a secret. Speaking of willies, I remember in a series later down the line we had a naked old fella on in a game called 'I'm coming'. Again it were like a game of 'Chicken'. I fink it may have been Gok Wan and Fearne that were playing... yeah it were. He were a right nice old man who I fought would meke a great Santa Claus if he'd put his cock away, but he insisted he weren't fat enough. Not sure how he knew how fat Santa's cock were. I remember Dan talking to me in me earpiece saying, 'slap his knob!' I fought 'how can I do this?' I dint wanna hurt him or really touch his dick to be honest. But I'm like Marty McFly in *Back t' Future*, when someone dares me to do somet or calls me 'chicken', I fall right into it. So I said, 'And the scores at the end of that round are... *Sha-ting!*' Then hit his knob.

'Ere's a bit of *Juice* trifia for ya. When I say 'Sha-ting' I mean it like the sound of a bell or a microwave when ya food is cooked. I don't mean 'Shitting', as in having a crap. It all came from the pilot in t' basement we shot. When I did the scores saying 'and the scores are' I asked will there be a sound effect there, so I just said 'Sha-ting' and rather than have a sound effect we just ended up with me just saying 'Sha-ting' and that's where that came from.

One of the stand-out moments that stands out for me were the time we had Dick and Dom on t' show so we had a kids TV theme show. The losing team got gunged and that week it were Fearne's team and she had Thomas Turgoose on, the little skin 'ed kid from that film/TV show *This is England*. I threw the bucket of gunge on 'em and proper went flying. Went for a right burton I did, smacking me head on t' floor. I fink I were out for t' count for about a second and when I got up I could see stars. I slurryly said, 'If I dint see ya through t' week I'll see ya through t' winda', a saying that me mate's mam use to say as I left his house when I were a kid and I'd been playing round there. Afterwards I were asked if I need to see a doctor cos I proper walloped me head. I said 'no', then about 20 minutes later I felt a bit odd and me head were killing. So the doc came to see me and I ended up in a neck brace for three days. Reminded meself of that old weirdo Merrion.

I fink *Celebrity Juice* gets better each series. The chemistry gets better and as a team we just get closer and closer. Me and Fearne often get off with each other at the wrap party – although she'll deny it cos she just can't remember as at the wrap party she just gets wrecked. It's not very often she goes but when she does she really enjoys herself and gets right pissed. Whereas

with Holly she gets pissed all t' time if she in't pregnant.
So as the show got more popular, I got invited onto
more shows and to more functions and stuff. I love
going to dos as I meet people that I never fought I'd
meet. Like Knight Rider, who's such a close personal
friend I can call him 'Dave' now.

Going to premieres is crazy, doing that whole red
carpet fing and people shouting ya name. Sometimes
I feel just like Rick Astley! And I promise I'm never
gonna give ya up, never gonna let ya down, never
gonna turn around and desert ya! That's a personal
message t' fans! I love you!

I did a podcast at some point again. While I were doing
the podcast I can remember not even really knowing
what one were. Still don't really. I invited me mate
Paloma t' studio for a chat and on the phone we had
Dermot O'Leary and me mam. We had to do a sound
check and I remember the sound engineer saying to
me, 'You just spoke non-stop for 72 minutes.' I weren't

sure if that were a long time or not enough. But the sound had been checked and we were ready to record. I dint fink too much would come of it cos as I said I dint really know what it were. But for the two podcasts that I did I won a Loaded Lafta award, which were great cos I got to meet Vic and Bob, who I fink are funny as fuck.

As I slowly became a face of the telly, I'd often go back to see me mates and me mam back in Leeds. Always got asked who I'd met especially by Rosie, who I'd see in t' pub. She always had time for me and I'd always have time for her cos I knew at the end of the night if I hadn't pulled, Rosie were a dead cert. I know that sounds arrogant of me. But I dint know back then what I know now. That why I put it about a bit. But I always used a rubber johnny cos me mate who lived life on t' edge more than I did never wore a johnny and once got some kinda STD and green pulp dispersed from his cock end. Said it stung like he were pissing nettles and I never wanted to feel that pain. He's right. No way!

I came back to London and I were asked to go on the ITV2 show *I'm a Celebrity Get Me Out of Here! NOW!* hosted by Caroline Flack, Joe Swash and Russell Kane, all guests on Juice. So, a trip to Oz to do a bit of telly with me mates. Fair dos. It took an effing lifetime to get there. 24 hours to be pecific. I fink I switched planes in Dubai. I would of missed me second plane, if it weren't for a nice bloke I'd met on t' flight who said he were a fan. I were a bit of a dingbat travelling by meself. Once I got out there it were great even though ya get picked up at 4am do a bit of telly. The other guests were Janet Street Porter, Mel Blatt, Donna Air and Scott Mills.

I mainly hung out with Flack and Blatt, both Bang Tidy. Mel Blatt is great for a piss up, which is all we did really. Eat pizza and get pissed. One day we went to somel called Movie World, I fink it were called. Did the funniest fing – we sat in a booth with a green screen cape wrapped around us so only our heads were showing. Then they keyed our head onto the bodies of some dancers dancing to Beyoncé. For $30 we all got a DVD of it each. We went back to Joe Swash's and watched it on a loop about 20 times pissing ourselves with both me and Joe finking any minute now one of 'em is gonna put their tits in our face. But it dint happen.

The following year I went out there again. I would of done again if I hadn't been busy shooting *Keith Lemon: The Film*. Craz-ey times. But before that I were gonna do my workout DVD with Lionsgate. And before that even, I were gonna perform a dirty dance for Comic Relief with Paddy McGuinness.

Dirty Dancing with Paddy

So I were sat watching telly one night. Not sure why I weren't doing out. I were just teking it easy on t' sofa, hands down me pants, twisting me ball sack with me fumb and forefinger. That's enough detail, I fink. Suddenly Paddy McGuinness calls me up. He always starts with somet funny – 'Now then ya cheeky badger', 'Ey up cockle', 'Ummm I like veins me, big blue veins'. So he tells me he's been asked to do a new show called *Let's Dance for Comic Relief* and that they're looking for celebrities to do classic dances from films. All I can fink is 'Me a celebrity?' Anywhere, he'd told 'em that he'd be up for it if I were and if we could do the last dance from *Dirty Dancing*, ya know the one with 'The Lift' at the end. It were nice to be asked to do somet for Comic Relief. I'd done a photoshoot for 'em the previous year, but they'd not asked me to do owt on t' telly. It's good to help out I fink and to have fun while doing it – well that's a bonus in't it. So, anywhere, I said yeah. I put the phone down and fought for a bit and then I fought, 'what have I just said "yeah" to?' So, I phoned Paddy back up and said, 'What are we doing again?'.

It weren't a simple sketch like I fought it were. No, of course not. They wanted us to properly learn the dance and perform it live in front of a studio audience – LIVE on t' telly. This were mini *Strictly Come Dancing* so it meant rehearsing everyday to compete in a competition against other celebrities. I panicked a bit, composed meself and fought, 'Well, as it's gonna help starving kids, it's a good fing to do.' And there's another

tip for ya: do a bit for charity and the girls will be putty in your hands.

Paddy started the rehearsals. He were the lead – Patrick Swayze – and I were 'Baby' – Jennifer Grey. If he were gonna be the lead, surely he needed more rehearsal than me and I'd just take his lead. I can dance a bit anywhere. As a child I use to dance as a means of communication as I cudn't speak till I were about eight. I were a wicked break dancer back then and I can still body pop like a good 'un. We were given two weeks rehearsal of which I missed the first five days cos of *Juice*. So when I joined Paddy, he already knew what we were doing. We did a run through and I fought, 'Fuck! I'm not gonna remember this.'

It were so odd dancing with a bloke, feeling his chunk on me thigh, and looking so closely and intensely into Paddy's eyes to replicate what they did in t' film. Ya can only imagine how many times we started laffing. First few days I hated it and suddenly, when the penny had dropped, I started to really enjoy it. We both did. We said the only way we're gonna win this fing were to fall in love but have no puffery. We rehearsed the shit out of it and word had started to spread that we were a bit good. Robert Webb (from *Peep Show*) had already won the first episode, which meant if we got through we would be competing against him in t' final. He were very good, performing the routine from *Flash Dance*. In our episode, me and Paddy were against Jo Brand (lovely woman, really liked her), The Dragons from *Dragons Den* (they were right nice, especially Peter Jones who later were a guest on *Juice* in which he got ripped for being an actual giant), Dr Fox (who in't really a 'Dr' or a 'fox') and Nancy Sorrell (Vic Reeves' incredibly fit wife, who is also a great singer).

There were also *Blue Peter* presenters, including Peter Duncan (Legend) and Janet Ellis (who's basically Sophie Ellis-Baxter but older. She'd get it, both of 'em would actually), Mark Kury (nice fella), Dianne-Louise Jordan (she were really nice), Anthea Turner (I fink she is so sexy, always liked her) and Helen 'Fit as Fuck' Skelton (fink she's brilliant, she's always doing great stuff for comic relief – I wonder if she'd like to do a sex tape with me for charity?).

I remember everyone sat backstage. All teking it far more serious than ya could ever imagine. None more than me and Paddy as we wanted to win like mad. Whenever we could, we just went through the routine. I can remember one night even practising it by meself in me garden. I dint know how many times I watched *Dirty Dancing* that week and I use to hate that film. Chick flick in't it? It's all about *Rocky*, *Rambo* and *Back t' Future* for me. We weren't too worried about the lift. That were the first fing we got down. Although if we'd have effed it up on the night it would've been a right shambles. That lift were our secret weapon. Paddy were in his Swayze get-up and he looked really good! I can remember moaning that my wig weren't the right colour. But the dress looked proper and I even had heels on. Those effing heels! Bastards, they were. They cut the shit outta me. But it finished the outfit off just right.

As the curtains went up, me and Paddy were sat at a table just finishing off our pints of lager. I picked up a watermelon and we walked on stage. Fink we were both shitting bricks. There were no choreographers there anymore to help us (and they were brilliant!). I dint fink we looked at anyfing or anyone else apart from each other's eyes. Just like Jonny and Baby in *Dirty Dancing*. All were going well, then came t' lift. We'd done it

We'd done it a thousand times and it cudn't go wrong while we're live on t' telly, could it? We were doing this for those starving kids after all! I shot up there like a majestic eagle and Paddy lifting me with all t' strength of the mighty Thor! Well, it weren't really like that, more like a short-arsed strawberry blond man in drag being lifted up by him from *Phoenix Nights*. I fink we pulled it off though. T' audience went mad. It were amazing. We dint really focus on anyfing else apart from each other. We stayed in character all the time and we got into trouble for the little kiss we did at the end. It were probably the most hormone sexual fing I'd ever done. Paddy had wanked someone off before, so it were nowt for him. Joking, Guinness!

We felt really chuffed with ourselves. Jo Brand came second which meant we both had a place in t' final. It were a good week that week. Had a lot of press and loads of hits on YouTube. I've always said it – I'm like a locket, I have a hard exterior but inside I'm soft and juicy, so it felt good to help out with Comic Relief. I were honoured and me mam were right proud.

In the final show, I fink we came on second. We fought, 'That's it then. We aren't gonna win.' And ya know what, we dint. But we had a great time at the wrap party and did the dance again, this time pissed up! Girls were queuing up for Paddy to lift 'em up, while I tried me best to get off with Claudia Winkleman.

After *Let's Dance* me and Paddy decided we should do some work together again. So we started writing stuff. We had an idea for a show recreating our favourite films on a budget. It were all inspired from the *Dirty Dancing* fing we did. So we wrote a half-hour version of *Dirty Dancing* called *Dirty Prancing*. We had a few meetings about it and it nearly happened but in the end it dint. I fink it would've been really good. We were gonna spoof a different film in each episode. It might happen one day but if it dint you'll find the first draft of the *Dirty Prancing* episode we wrote together at t' end of book.

Keith Lemon's FIT

S **o with my dancing career behind me,** I had a bit
more time to focus on finally getting me film off
the ground. I got invited to a Lionsgate premiere so I
went along with a mate from me Leeds massive. It were
Sunday, I fink, and it were the premiere of a film called
Righteous Kill starring Al Pacino and Robert DeNiro. I
like 'em two. Pecifically Pacino in his Carlito formation
and DeNiro as Rupert Pupkin in the cult classic *King
of Comedy*. It's ace! I like *Taxi Driver* as well. When he
makes a gun holster fing that shoots out of his wrist,
out of a bit of sofa... Imagine 'em showing ya how to do
that on *Blue Peter*. Janet Ellis eat ya heart out. '*Yo yo
yo! Welcome to a special mutha fuckin' Bronx edition
of Blue PetOR. Check this. This week we're gonna be
showing y'all how to make a bad ass projectile gun
holster that pops out of your sleeve like some terminator
shit right there. Y'all know what I'm talking about. You
dig? But first, here's what happened when one of my main
brothas went kayaking down some white water rapid shit.
That dude be ruthless! Let's see what went down...*'

Anywhere, me mate Paul had never been to a premiere
before so took advantage of the free bar at the after
show party. Why not? I bumped into an old friend of
mine that I hadn't seen in some time and he told me
that Lionsgate were gonna be meking his next film.
I actually dint know he'd made one before. In fact, he
hadn't. It were gonna be his first. But he knew how to
talk fings up. That were one of his talents. A bit like
me. It's not lying, it's enhancing the truth to meke

for good pub chat and for chatting up the ladies of course. Anywhere, I were right happy for him and he introduced me to his acquaintance at Lionsgate.

Paul said that me and him should meke a film! I said, 'Yeah I'd love to meke a film.' I'd always fancied meself as the next Owen Wilson. Get told I look like him except me nose in t' shaped like a penis. So we chatted about t' film for a while and kept on getting more and more excited. Then me attention were drawn to a certain Katie Price that were sat in t' corner. I said to me mate, 'Don't look now but that Katie Price is over there.' So what did he do? He looked now.

I forgave him cos as I said he'd never been to a premiere before and he dint realise ya have to play it all cool. It's like when you're on t' beach with your bird and you're checking out all t' other ladies with dark glasses on. To be honest though, I fink he were more bothered that the drinks were free and that they were serving these tiny, tiny burgers and fish and chips that were so tiny it were like they'd had a shrinking serum injected into them. Imagine, a whole burger in one bite. It blew his tiny little mind. Between us we must 'ave polished off about 15 of those little bastards.

It were a great night and nice to see me old mate Paul. We stumbled out of the party pissed up and full of tiny burgers and carefully looked for a place to have a slash without getting caught by the law. I were finking it were the best outside piss of me life, until I looked up to find that I were pissing against a police station. With the speed of haste, I shook it and put it away and speeded off. Then, by the Wednesday I were in Lionsgate having a meeting about doing a film. Cudn't believe it. Keith Lemon in glorious flat 2D.

I sometimes get asked who would play me in a film about me. It's like when ya go to a super hero film, the question ya most often get asked is, 'What power would ya have if ya were a super hero?' I always say the power of flight – although once when I appeared on *Richard Bacon's Beer and Pizza Club,* I said me power would be to shoot Scotch eggs from the palm of me hand. I fink a projectile Scotch egg in the face would hurt but it wun't kill me nemesis, cos if you're a super hero and ya kill someone you've crossed over t' dark side. But that's irrelevant, in't it? What is relevant is who would play me in a film about me? Erm... I would, of course! And that's the plan.

We had meeting after meeting developing the story for the film. Scriptwriting lasted almost three years. That's not solid writing obviously. I were doing plenty of other fings while it were going on. But the basic premise for t' film were it were to be an origin sort of fing.

So whenever I were filming *Juice,* or doing whatever, I were also writing the film that I never actually fought would happen. But it were through the film meetings that another project came about. One day in a meeting, a Bang Tidy bird from another department came in and said they had two more DVD entities left, and would I be interested in meking a workout DVD? I weren't sure what an 'entity' were apart from I'd seen a film called *The Entity,* where a woman were getting molested by a ghost. Horrible film, I hoped it weren't gonna be anyfing like that. But I sure as hell knew what a workout DVD were as I'd wanked off to so many when I were a kid. So, I considered it for less than a short second and then said, 'Yeah! I'm up for a workout DVD.'

I know I don't have the body of a god but I am fast. I'm robust. It mekes a lot of sense me doing a workout DVD because people will listen to me because I've got me own problems too just like everyone else. Well, I haven't really but sometimes I wear a verucca sock at the swimming pool – I don't have a verucca, I just want to look normal.

All I could fink of when I fought of this workout DVD were that music video of Eric Prydz's 'Call On Me' with that F.A.F. bird with the naughty body. What if I could do my workout video with her? That'd be worth doing. That video were amazing. More amazing than meat and po-ta-to pie! Don't know if ya've seen that video, but basically they're all fit and wearing 80s gym gear. A great video to pump fist to if you're away travelling and have got no babe station – apart from there's a man in t' video, but just block him out with ya mind.

Anywhere, if I were gonna do a fitness video, she were the perfect girl to do it with. So they got in touch with her, Deanne Berry her name were. Deanne is Australian for Diane. Now that woman has an arse! You'd let her use your face as toilet paper. You'd let her fart in your face. It is proper incredible! She were interested in doing it and came in for a meeting. Now I'm not gonna name names cos I don't wanna embarrass anyone – ya know who ya are, and ya know what I mean – but when she came in there weren't a bloke in that room that could stand up. And this were her just in normal clothes, not even the leotard fong fing she wears in t' video which we were obviously gonna get her to wear in our DVD – *Keith Lemon's Fit.*

She were actually right nice. I had no idea how to meke a workout DVD so I asked 'er to drag in some of 'er mates and basically she led and I followed. That's why I dint bother going to the rehearsal. So the weekend before we were shooting it – in the exact location used in t' Eric Prydz video – I popped up to Leeds to see me pals and a certain Rosie Parker.

While in Leeds, me mate Paul were badgering me to get him on t' telly. I told him when the time were right I'd try. He's like a mini Alexei Sayle crossed with Bruce Willis. He is right funny, though.

Had a good chat with Rosie about how fings had changed in me life. She never seemed like one of those birds that were interested in me just cos I were on telly, and there were a lot of those, and I can't lie, sometimes ya just fink, 'Bollox let's have a go. If she wants to go around telling everyone she's had some Lemon juice then so be it.'

Rosie's different though. I'd often end up with a cheeky snog at the end of the night and then some. But I never wanted to say she were me bird, even though she were acting like me bird a bit. But we never said we were 'boyfriend and girlfriend'. I fink she knew that I wanted to get out there and explore before I settled with one lass. I were a lot naughtier back then.

Anywhere, it were Monday and I were back in London to do the workout DVD. It were gonna be a two-day shoot. Two days of dancing around with sweaty F.A.F. dancers. Every single one of 'em were fit. In me head, I fought the kids are gonna love this. I wanted it to be like an old school workout DVD that young lads could watch when their parents were out. It were me gift to 'em before they got into pumping fist over porn. I'm not right into porn meself, but I much prefer softer stuff such as a workout DVD or somet like *Basic Instinct*. After two days of dancing around I were proper fucked, but it were a lot of fun.

If you're wondering about the secret to my great body, I'll tell ya. I've been working on the theory that it's all about quantities, in't it. For example, I believe in binge drinking. I fink to binge drink is better than drinking shit loads every night. I know that scientists say to have a glass of wine a day but don't binge. But what a waste of time! You're not gonna get pissed as a newt like that are ya? I say, save it all for Saturday night and get hammered.

Anywhere, while this were happening I were still writing the film with Paul the Director. I'd just stand up and walk around sensationalising fings that had happened to me in real life, adding total fabrication for the purpose of filmic entertainment. When we laffed, then that'd go down in t' script. It were a lot different approach to working on *Celebrity Juice*. I write nowt for *Juice*, just turn up, have a drink and a laff. I've always said that I fink the success behind *Juice* is that folk like to watch us enjoying ourselves. The day we're not enjoying it anymore is the day we should stop doing it. But I fink we all still really enjoy it.

When my fitness DVD came out, I remember it being number one in the Fitness chart on Amazon, while Davina McCall were number six. I were a bit embarrassed by that, cos Davina's were a proper workout DVD and mine were just a bit of fun.

I really enjoyed doing the promotion for the DVD as Deanne did a lot with me. It were nice doing it with someone rather than by meself. It's like sex in't it? A wank is fun, but it's more fun when someone is doing it for ya. Sometimes I wish I were doing it with her. Boy, she were fit.

We did magazine stuff together – *Nuts* and *Zoo* and stuff. *Love It* mag were a funny one. We had photos done around the *Love It* van and they'd interview us as though we were in the van, but the interview were actually in an office. Not sure if you've ever read *Love It*, but there's a lot of sad tragic stories, then an interview with a celebrity. For example, in this week's *Love It*, there's a woman, pregnant with twins, involved in a punch up; there's the guilt of a mother that fell in love with a pedo; an interview with Abbey Clancy, who's 'skinny, but not happy' and the chance to win a trip to Alton Towers for four! What's not to love about *Love It*?!

We were also asked to perform a routine from the DVD at T4's Stars of 2010, which were a lot of fun. To start with, I were gonna be sharing a dressing room with five Bang Tidy birds. Result! And there were lots of stars there – The Saturdays, Olly Murs, Alexandra Burke, Example, Pixie Lott (best legs ever) and Professor Green. It were a big event! We had to show the producers the routine before we actually performed it, but apparently it were too rude and what the girls were wearing were not enough so we had to change it for a T4 audience. No thrusting. No thrusting, me arse! We did it anyhow and got away with it.

I remember I had to shoot some pre-title sketches before it with Frankie from t' Saturdays, Alexandra Burke and maybe Olly Murs. It were the first time I heard the phrase 'You is jokes' from Alexandra Burke. Fink that's her street lingo for 'Hey, you're right funny you!' Keeping it real, see! All in all I fink it worked. I'd done T4 stuff in t' past and there's always a worry that ya not gonna be able to say or do what ya want cos it's a younger audience. But I'd trained meself when to rude it up and when not to. I never swore or owt in front of me mam. In fact, t' first time me mam heard me swear were on t' telly. Never swore in front of her. Respect, in't it? She knows a lot of what I say on telly is just for jokes. And as Alexandra Burke says, I am 'jokes', an't I?

I never had it off with Deanne Berry. Dint even cup her tits in t' end. Oh, actually, I may have cupped her tits. But she had a boyfriend and were planning to get married. So, while she fucked off back to Australia, I continued to do PR for the DVD. I were doing a signing at an ASDA in Derby and I'd seen Katie Price do her signing on t' telly at the same ASDA and it were packed. I were worried I'd not be as popular but in t' end I signed for three hours, so it were a good turnout and everyone were happy.

Then I were asked to present 'behind the scenes' at the Comedy Awards with the lovely Emma Willis. I weren't nominated for one so I fought, 'Fuck it! Yeah, I'll do it!' I know Emma and she's lovely. I'd been on *Big Brother's Little Sister's Uncle*, or whatever they were calling it then. Emma hosted it with George Lamb. Another top bloke and I'd say, apart from me, the best-dressed man on telly. George's been on *Juice*, but to this day I dint know why Emma hasn't been on. Not sure if ya follow me on Twittor @lemontwittor, but as I say on there, *I DON'T BOOK THE GUESTS*. I'm forever being asked when will One Direction be on? When will Lady GaGa be on? When is Jessie J on? When's Rihanna on? Hey, they're all welcome! But it an't up to me!

And you, too, Gary Barlow! Who apparently is a big fan of the show. I've recently struck up a text friendship with him. I'd only spoken to him via text, until a few weeks ago, when he agreed to do a cameo in the film. Right nice fella he is and I'd love for him to come on *Juice*. Imagine that – a Take That Special! You can only hope. As I said... *I DON'T BOOK THE GUESTS*.

157

Speaking of Twittor, let's have look at some of me most recents. This is a shout out to all ya tweeters! Fanks for all your support. I hope there's no horrible ones like the one I had the other day. A young girl wanted to throw a brick in me face. Don't know what I'd done to upset her. Bint.

audra armsden @lemontwittor god,what a guy,celeb juice, lemonaid, and your film, now a book whens that out is it about you? any juicey goss in it lol xxx

That's nice, in it! Yeah, the book is about me and if you've bought it, you'll know it's about me. Cheers for buying it!

Tiff Foster @lemontwittor its me birthday today, could I have a RT please so I can brag :-)

Get these all the time too. 'Appy birfday Tiff!

louise jacobs @Nandos_Official I'm on the case of the renewal of @lemontwittor nandos card seein as it were said on national radio that he'd b getin a new1

That's nice, too. I said on Chris Moyles' Radio show that me Nando's card had run out. I use to be the Chicken Master!

It's really odd when ya get angry tweets from bitter people. I don't know how they can be arsed. Sometimes I wanna retaliate and tell 'em I hope they get impetigo all around their mouth and eyes or their dick falls off or they get mutilated by a fox or they get some sort of minge infection. But I'm just not that angry. I'm nice me! And niceness works! Just the other day I got some free shoes cos I'm nice and if being nice gets ya free shoes then I'm sticking with nice!

Working with Emma Willis were really nice. I fink she gets me sense of humour. She weren't scared of me or anyfing. A lot of people get all scared. I don't know what they fink I'm gonna do. But Emma were really cool. I'd like to work with her again or at least have a hand job from her if fings go wrong with Rosie. Emma's got the craziest blue eyes, beautiful.

It were a little odd interviewing a load of drunken comedians that I knew. It were funny running into Kevin Bishop. He's a good lad. We had a cheese throwing competition. Well, I say 'competition', but it weren't really. I just asked Kevin if he fancied throwing owt as the previous year I fink he were a little drunk and decided to throw fings. All in jest though. He's a top bloke (I know him even better now after t' film). So, we threw a bit of cheese on't stage.

The highlight though were meeting Pamela Anderson for the first time. Little did she (or I) know that she'd be a guest on *Juice* in t' future doing a pole dance for me. Incredible! I honestly can't believe me life sometimes. There I am sat in front of t' telly, eating a packet of crabsticks, the next minute I'm looking into Pamela Anderson's eyes finking, 'Ya know what love, you're aging pretty well! I'd love to meke vigorous love to ya.'

I fink we all do that with people we fancy. We shake their hands and say 'How do', and then we imagine 'em naked and before ya know it, we're smashing their back doors in, their front doors, maybe even in t' mouth... Sometimes I say too much me. Me mates say it's like an evil wizard has injected me with a truth serum. If I offend, I never mean to. I just fink honesty is the best policy. And from experience, if ya say everyfing with a cheeky nod and a wink, nine times outta ten ya get away with it!

My pulling methods are more maturer these days. Before I were like 'Hi, I'm Keith Lemon, wanna fuck?' but now I get 'em to notice me much more subtle like. Ya can tell if someone fancies ya, they'll look ya straight in t' eye. And what I'll do is, I'll stare back, trying to intimidate them a bit, not looking away, not even to look at all t' other fit birds. I always do that. I can remember one of the researchers on *Lemonaid* who were a body double for Jennifer Aniston in the film *Derailed* and I did it to her and she goes 'Stop it!' and I'm acting all innocent like, 'Stop what?' and she's like, 'You know what you're doing!' And I did cos I were gazing into her eyes like a predator, not like a *sexual* predator, more like a really focused leopard. She were dead attractive but I didn't act on it because I had a bird already. And I've changed that way. Faithful you know.

Before Rosie moved in, I were faithful but not as faithful as I am now. If she caught me cheating though she'd understand cos she knows that it's hard for me because I have so many women throwing themselves at me feet. It's hard, and sometimes I'm weak. But if I'm flirting too much, she'll drag me away. We had a dinner party a couple of weeks ago, Stacey Soloman were there, Chris Fountain, Toby Anstis and Jenny Powell. And Jenny Powell fancies me, that is scientific fact, and when she kissed me goodbye I got sucked in dint I, and kissed her a bit more than I should've and Rosie fucking dragged me off and then just snogged my face to bits in front of Jenny Powell then said 'Goodbye,

Jenny Powell'. I said to Toby, 'You better go, cos we're gonna have sex' and he told us to get a room but we already had one cos it were our house and every room were ours. Good night that.

Just had a little break and watched some Jessie J clips on YouTube. Very rare a bird looks fit even without make up. I fink she's lovely Jessie J – and she can sing like a bastard! Proper good singer. I had a dream about her a few weeks ago. Boy, she were naughty. Not sure it's true or not I heard see were bisensual? Whatever. Even if she's full blown lesbican. She's ace! Cool as Fuck and Super Bang! Fink she's me new favourite.

Ask Uncle Keith

Fings cun't have been going more betterer when I got a call asking me if I wanted to do a weekly slot on *This Morning* as an Agony Uncle. Of course, I did! I love *This Morning* and the fact that Holly's on it made it even more attractiverer – we could go into work together in the morning after the night before. And I know some fings about life and its problems. I've got a gay brother and had a fucked up toe before, so I were well up for it and more than qualified. I'm like a wise owl.

The first week I did it, I could see the worry in Uncle Philip's eyes. But I fink Holly must've reassured him that I'm not a mental. It went really well. I really enjoyed helping people with their problems. I fink I actually really helped them. Here's a sample of me wise pearls.

AGONY UNCLE KEITH'S ADVICE

If your boyfriend in t' giving ya the attention ya fink ya deserve then trade him in get a new 'un.
If your wife finks you're cheating, hey go ahead and cheat! She finks ya are anywhere, so ya may as well give her somet to be suspicious about.
If ya can't lose weight stop being a salad dodger, maybe get one of those elastic bands on your arse like Fearne Britton did. She looks well on it!

I did the Agony Uncle stuff for a while and then I went onto reviewing fings such as bouncy water slides and trampolines. The girl I were doing that item with were F.A.F. I suggested to her that later that afternoon I went round hers to see how bouncy her bed were!

I also do a bit of cooking sometimes with me mate Gino D'Acampo. We made a peach Alaska in Christmas jumpers, it were ace! Gino's a great cook and I like the way he tries to put a naughty word in 'ere and there. Never says 'couldn't', it always sounds like a naughty four letter word. Similar to me accent. I always say 'cudn't'. 'He could but ya cudn't!'

Jenny Powell were there one week, too. She's F.A.F! I fancied Jenny Powell for years. It's strange cos she looks a bit like Michael Jackson but also like a super fit, Bang Tidy bird. I'd let her kick the shit out of me and I'm not really into that kinda fing as ya know. I gave her the eye and flirted with her but I dint do owt. Fings had started getting serious with Rosie. Again, we never said we were an item, but it were blossoming into somet and I fink we both knew it. So out of respect for Rosie, I never touched Jenny Powell. But in me mind, I finger blasted her to bits.

JENNY OR IS IT MJP

Sometimes I did *This Morning* on a Friday with Ruth and Eamonn, when Phil and Holly weren't there. They're all right nice down at *This Morning*, which is why I enjoyed doing it. Alison Hammond is always nice to cuddle, Dr Chris is a lovely man and I class Gino as one of me pals. Phil Vickery's always nice to me, too. I always end up hanging out in t' pub when I'm down there, whether it's with Coleen Nolan (bet she gives a good blow job, massive bangers!), Stephen Mulhern (that evil wizard can pull a wine bottle out of a napkin, fuck knows how he does it), Matt Johnson (lovely Welsh bloke, nearly as good looking as me) or lovely Samantha (quiet at first, but ya know what they say about the quiet ones).

Sharon Marshall's always good for a bit of crack, too. I shared a cab home with her from the NTAs. I won't say what went on cos I don't wanna wreck her marriage, just that she's *very* giving. I were at the NTAs with *This Morning*. I felt a bit of a dingbat, to be honest, cos I'd only just started working there and there I were hanging out with 'em all like I'd been doing it for ages. But they invited me and what a great night it were. I bumped into someone who knew me old pal Patsy Kensit. When I say 'old', I don't mean she's old. Cos if she starts reading this, she'll get a complex, finking she's old. She looks as fit now as she did when she use to meke records, back in t' past. I only bought her records to put the cover up on me Wank Wall. Although I did like one of her songs 'I'm Not Scared'. I fink she does a French version of that song. Very sexy.

Yeah, it were a fantastic night. I remember when they announced *This Morning* as the winners and I went up with the team. They told me to!

When I were up there even me mate Dermot O'Leary said, 'What you doing up 'ere?'

So I said, 'I do *This Morning* now, don't I?'

I could see the look of disbelief in his eyes so I said, 'Watch this.'

Then I just stepped in between Uncle Phil and Holly and smiled right at the camera while they did their speech. I were basically looking at all me mates and Rosie and me mum to say, 'Look at me at the NTAs! Effing madness. I cudn't believe it.'

It almost felt like ITV had embraced me. I hope they're still embracing me when this books out and I an't been given the boot cos I've said somet I shun't. Cos that's what I always feel like when I'm on live telly. Any minute I'm just gonna shout, *'Your mam's a slag!'* And it'll be all over. Maybe I have got a mild case of Tourette's. Any commissioners reading this, don't worry I'll never shout 'Your mam's a slag!', I promise. But, yeah, I felt part of ITV and felt even more a part of it when the asked me to host a Saturday night show called *Sing If Ya Can*. Ooooosh! Lemon on primetime!

Sing If Ya Can

Anywhere, I get a call from me agent, George, who is fit as is her assistant Lara and they're both very good at their jobs. I love introducing 'em to blokes. Ya can see it straight away in their eyes, 'Ya said that your agent were fit, but I dint believe ya.' Well, believe it! Me Reps are fit boi. I'd destroy 'em both, but it would ruin our working relationship. And mine with Rosie. Oh, and their's with their other halfs. So let's just all keep it professional and keep the sex part in our minds, right George? She wants me so bad. One day I met up with her for a meeting and she had a bandage on her hand. Gave me some nonsense about a car accident. She wants me so bad, she wants to be me! I'm joking. Sort of – ish.

So, I get this call. ITV have done this pilot and want me to be a judge on the panel. I said, 'Yeah, why not?' Then they asked if I would be a judge every week? I weren't 100% sure but I fought it might be good for a laff.

Anywhere, I got another call a few days later just after I'd been having me barnet done (just a few highlights to enhance me strawberry blondness) and this time I were being asked by me fit agent if I'd *host* the show. I were flattered, of course, but I were also curious. In the pilot, Vernon Kay were the host. So what had happened? And I cudn't possibly do it like Vernon, we're different animals. If we actually were animals he'd be a giraffe and I'd be a Jack Russell that's how different we are. The show were a format that already existed. A crazy singing show in which celebrity contestants sang to win money for charity. They showed me the pilot,

Vernon's a giraffe and I'm a jack russell

but not the bits with Vernon in. Not sure why. It looked a right laff. Later Vernon told me, while he were in t' dressing room about to be a guest on *Juice*, that it were him that suggested me to do it. Which I fought were right nice of him. What a lovely lanky Bolton bastard he is. Vernon's a top lad. All t' best Vernon!

So me co-host on the show were gonna be none other than sexy Stacey Soloman. All I knew of Stacey were she were a good singer. I'd seen her on *The X Factor*, which is one of me favourite shows, and I'd seen her eat a kangaroo's pink bits on *I'm a Celebrity Get Me Out of Here!*, one of me other favourite shows, so I knew she were gonna be up for a laff.

The show were being shot at Pinewood Studios. So, cos I dint know her that well, I made a point of befriending her as quick at possible. As soon as I got there, I went to Stacey's trailer and said 'How do!, I'm not leaving till ya know everyfing about me and I know everyfing about ya. I'm circumcised and this is what it looks like. Smooth as a dolphin's beak. Do dolphins have beaks? Who cares! Now show me ya big hangers!'

So I made a point of becoming her friend right quickly so once we got in front of the cameras we would get on and have wicked chemistry. She is lovely and before ya could say sexy Soloman I were calling her names and we were the best of mates. I remember her telling me she fought she had rodent like features so from then on I called her a 'Sexy Rat'. She has a great sense of humour. Did I already mention she has great bangers, too? Well she does...

I fink this were her first big presenting gig and it were me first time doing family entertainment. We were happy with it and the audience figures were great but it did get a bit of a slagging. I knew it would cos it were fun and silly. Great Saturday night telly. It were mad as fuck. I remember Sinitta were on it. She came on in a wheelchair cos she'd done her leg in and sang, 'So macho', while being rained on. Hailstone, bricks, snow, all sorts of shit were thrown at her. Jedward were on as well. They had what looked like tar poured on 'em while they were singing. They're nuts those two!

It were off its 'ed and the response to it were cut right down t' middle. Like I said, the ratings were good but a couple of critics slagged it off. Anywhere they're paid to be nasty, I guess. I always fink of critics as panto baddies. Boo, hissss! Panto baddies that are too scared to be guests on *Celebrity Juice*!

Got to meet a lot of nice people on *Sing If Ya Can*. One of me favourite judges on it had to be Sarah Cox. She's really funny and got the show immediately. Big up ya chest, Sarah Cox! I fink everyone that were involved in it enjoyed it anywhere.

Living by The Rules

It **were a busy time.** While *Sing If Ya Can* were going, *Celebrity Juice* were still on. Then I were asked to write a book. I honestly cun't believe what were going on. How mad it were! Still can't. Can't believe I'm writing this second one now. But, I'd always wanted to write a book. I'd had a lot of experience with ladies so I fought it'd be good to share me knowledge of the opposite sex and the same sex. I asked me brother for his tips on that sort of fing. I comprised all those facts in a little red pocket-size book called *The Rules, 69 Ways To Be Succ-sex-ful.* Oooooosh!

Me book

Right I might go have somet to eat now. I'm starving. Gotta write me *Now* magazine column, too! In't that funny that I have a column in *Now* magazine. It's proper like me diary. Is very liberating to look back and see what I were up to. I dint keep a diary when I were a lad. I had a great Black Book though, full of fit women. It were me Wank Book! Should publish that! Anywhere, I'm gonna go have me dinner, then I fink I'm going out with Rosie, who will remind not to put too much explicit info in her about me and her. I'll not write owt.

Be back in a bit...

How do! Well, it's a new day. A sunny one at last – but the weather has been shite. Of course, the day it's finally sunny, I'm sat in an office writing, when I could be outside in t' sun checking out the totty. Just looking at it, Rosie.

Anywhere, just to update ya on what I've been up to since I last wrote, a few days ago I met up with me old mate Caroline Flack and we went to meet Jack Osbourne, who'd made a documentary about his dad. Proper good it were. Maybe I should meke a documentary about me dad, ya know The Great Billy Ocean. Hopefully, we gonna be doing a remix soon of 'When the Going Gets Tough' for t' end credits of *Keith Lemon: The Film* and I fink I might be doing some rapping on it, with special guest Rizzle Kicks. I hope it happens, I fink it will be ace!

Since I wrote anyfing last, I've been doing a photoshoot for a fancy fashion magazine called *Rollercoaster*. Right posh clobber it were, ya know Versace, Prada, Dolcy and Cabanna. On this photoshoot I had Jay Jay (or Justine) with me. She's the make-up lady from *Celebrity Juice*, who does Fearne a lot. She's got her work cut out when she's with Fearne though with those massive nostrils. Anywhere I were telling her about me book and she said, 'Have ya mentioned me in it?' I said, 'Yeah I fink so.' But I cun't remember if I have so I'm mentioning her now. Jay Jay is right good at make-up. She's a lovely woman that dresses like she's from the past. Wears all that 50s clobber. Looks good though. She's right good at her job and has massive bangers that she likes to press upon me while she's trowelling on me clart. I always ask for 2% less on me clarted-up face than Jodie Marsh to meke me look healthy. She does a grand job! Cheers Jay Jay.

So all were going well and I were working on me first book. I wanted to have lots of pictures, cos to be honest I dint read a lot of books. In fact, the only books I've read are film books – *Rambo*, *Return of t' Jedi*, *Gremlins*, *Lost Boys* and *Back t' future*. All of which have glossy photos in t' middle. So I'd read up t' pictures and often never the rest. Not sure why I dint just jump t' pictures in t' middle; I fink it were cos I'd paid for t' book.

I don't read a lot but I've read Geri Halliwell's book from t' Spice Girls. Fink I picked that up at an airport. Hey, she's had some hard times her. Lived in a squat and everfing apparently. So, well done her for doing so well now. I use to fancy her a bit. Not when she went all fin, I prefer her when she's carrying a bit of timber. Her bangers look betterer... I wish she'd come on *Celebrity Juice* though. I fink she'd be a good guest.

So once I'd written *The Rules*, which were published by Orion, the same people that've published this 'un, (they're all nice and have some tidy birds there too), I were asked to do all t' drawings for it (like this one). I right enjoyed it cos I fought if there's any people that have bought the book but cudn't read well, they can just look at the pictures. Some of them I did on me iPad, although not many of them were used. I love drawing on me iPad, although people often don't believe that I've done 'em. There's a popular miss conception that I'm fick. But I know some fings and I know how to do right nice pictures on me iPad! At one point I wanted to do an exhibition of me iPad art, but that were one of those fings that dint happen. So have a look at some over t' page.

Anywhere, before too long I were back on t' road again, this time doing some book signings for *The Rules*. There were a few dates in London, where I bumped into an old pal of mine, Cleo Rocos from t' *Kenny Everett Show*, which I use to love when I were a kid. I remember Kenny doing a sketch where he were Spiderman and cudn't find his fly so he ended up pissing himself. I've known Cleo ages and she speaks like no one else I know. She don't say 'I'm off for me haircut', she says 'I'm off for me hairs cut'. I'll say 'Ya "hairs"? Dint ya mean ya "hair"? She'll say, "Well no, because there are many of them, so surely it's "hairs"?' She's got a point I guess.

Then I went onto t' Bluewater shopping centre. It's always a bit scary doing a signing cos ya don't know if anyone's gonna turn up, but in t' end it were a great turnout. I'd say an even better turnout than when I were signing me fitness DVD. But nofing would prepare me for going back up t' North. It were total madness there. I felt like Harry Styles from One Erection. They had barriers up, massive bouncers and everyfing. Of course, some old school mates popped down and me mam, of course. I were a bit disappointed that Rosie dint come though. I fought she would've.

It were Halloween when I were up so I were in costume. Of course I like to embrace the festivities so I dressed as the Joker – Heath Ledger's Joker to be pecific. I looked The Dog's Bollox. I remember bumping into Batman and Robin on a train platform. Oh aye, I were dressed up on t' train! It were great as people dint recognise me as much. I were in Glasgow, Liverpool and then Manchester and people were right nice, giving me gifts and stuff. Including a beautiful pair of knitted bangers that I then gave to Fearne on *Celebrity Juice*. Better to have knitted bangers than no bangers! A lot of people asked me to sign their potatoes or lemons, as well as the book. Not sure what they'd want with an old mouldy potato or lemon with me name on, but I did it anywhere.

Somebody even gave me a silver leather jacket, which had the words 'Mr Lover Man, Mot, Mot, Mot' written on t' back. I wore that on *Celebrity Juice* that week. That were the first episode that we introduced 'Indian Keith', who's actually a Geordie. Yeah, I really enjoyed those signings, although me hand hurt after cos I had to sign me name I don't know how many times.

Keith Lemon: The Film

So, now I had a travel show out, *Celebrity Juice* were in its sixth series and I'd won a Loaded Lafta and a TV Choice Award. I'd written a book and now finally, after many rewrites, three years of development and thousands of meetings, we'd got the green light to actually go ahead and shoot a film.

I kept finking about all those telly appearances and red carpet moments where I'd spoke about meking a film. I swear people fought it were just part of me banter. 'Yeah! Yeah! I'm meking a film. Look at me.' But it were true; I were gonna actually be in a film that'd be at the cinema!

I'd not worked on the film script for a few months cos I'd been busy taking the piss out of Dot Cotton on *Juice* and promoting me book. But it were good that *Juice* were on air cos it gave me more of a sense of what the tone for the film should be like. I told Paul the Director that we had to give it far more edge, rude it up like.

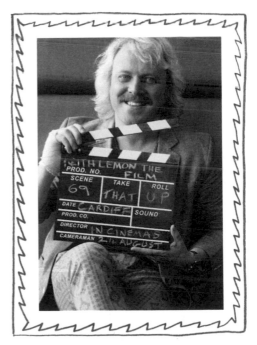

Anywhere, I hadn't seen what Paul the Director had done to the film script, but it were already being sent out to potential cast members as I found out when I had a call from Holly Willoughbooby.

She said, 'I've just received a copy of your film script.'

I said, 'Oh aye?'

She said, 'You know I'd do owt for you...' (She wun't though, she'd never suck me off while tickling me balls and letting me seagull her bangers.) 'But I can't do this. It's disgusting!'

I said, 'Hold on! I aint seen *this* version!'

Turns out, when I told Paul to 'rude it up', he had got a little bit carried away and turned it into a porno! When I finally saw it, I said t' him I weren't happy and I wanted to rewrite it. And that's what we ended up doing like, just three days before shooting it. We also still had no cast.

In the film I have a girlfriend called Rosie. It were loosely based on Rosie, me on-and-off bit on t' side that were a bit more than just a bit on t' side. So we had to find a girl to play her. Originally Paloma Faith were gonna play her, but she were tied up with work and cun't do it. What a bastard, as who were now gonna play Rosie? Lots of girls auditioned and there were one girl that in me mind were perfect! Only problem were she looked nowt like Rosie. She were a big black lass and it just dint look right. She were about seven-feet tall. I looked like a hobbit next to her.

So, after finking I said I know someone who can play Rosie better than anyone. Me Rosie from Leeds, of course.

Rosie as Rosie

But there were lots of concerns that she weren't an actress though. She weren't, but it seemed silly to me cos she dint need to be. She were gonna be playing herself, just like I were playing meself. I weren't totally sure she'd do it though. She weren't really one for t' limelight. But I fought I'd ask her and all seemed right. Maybe this were all meant to be, after all t' others that I'd been sticking it in over the years some of them were right dirty.

We were supposed to be shooting in a few weeks time so I legged it up to Leeds and arranged to meet Rosie, who were temping at time. We met up in a wine bar, I fink it were, in t' centre of town. She looked Bang Tidy. She always does. She looked... like she should be in a film. Me film! So I just asked her. Initially, she weren't keen. She'd lived in Leeds all her life and I don't fink she'd ever even been to London. And she'd seen the looks that people from *Emmerdale* get when they walk in pubs in Leeds. People would look at them like 'Who do they fink they are? I bet they fink they're somet, them.' I'd fought it meself to be honest. It might not be like that now but it certainly were back then.

That's why I were chuffed the first time I went back to Leeds after I'd been on t' telly and I dint get that. I were expecting that glare though, that 'D'ya tink ya Billy Big Bollox now cos you've been on t' telly?' glare. Luckily everyone just wanted to buy me pints. Which most of t' time I accepted.

So I told her it wun't be acting cos she'd just be playing herself. More than that, if it all went well she could be playing with me too! All t' years when we'd just have a bit of slap and tickle at the end of t' night. I said to her, 'Why don't we kinda date properly and see how it goes?'. Sure, it were gonna be odd for her. I were now as famous as probably Richard Bacon and I had a Nando's card just like he did. When ya got that black Nando's card, ya know ya cudn't be doing too bad. I told her that we were gonna be shooting in Belfast, so whatever temp work she had she'd have to drop and go there with me – that is, if she were up for it. She said she'd fink about it.

All I could fink were, 'What's there to fink about? D'ya wanna be in a film? D'ya wanna be me girlfriend in me film and maybe be me girlfriend in real life if the spark is there like I fink it might be?' I know everytime I came back to Leeds, she were giving me t' eye. Maybe she dint want people finking she were just going out with me cos I were on telly… I dint know.

Anywhere, I went back to London on t' Sunday and on t' Monday morning Rosie called and said she were up for it. At last, I had someone to play Rosie, and also I were gonna have a proper grown-up relationship, but this were gonna be odd. Especially as in t' film I have two girlfriends and t' other were gonna be the FAFest of all t' FAF birds. I'd go so far as t' say The Fittest Girl in The UK and Woman of Me Dreams Kelly Brook! Super Bang!

Then, somet happened in the time before I went to Belfast to shoot the cleverly entitled *Keith Lemon: The Film*. I'd been asked to feature in… wait for it an ad for… wait for it… *ADIDAS!* So, I said 'Yeah' straight away and went along for a meeting with Lara, one of me fit agents, to see a fella called Steve. Top bloke he were and looked like Spiderman. Right nice and all. Told me about all these Olympians that I knew nowt about that I'd be interviewing. He also told me about 'finger blasting'. Which I also knew nowt about at time, but is a term I've used ever since, including 'ere in this book already. If ya dint know what it means let me tell ya what it means. What it means is meking love with ya finger vigorously with the speed of haste! Simple as peas. Everyfing in me life right now were moving at that same speed, the speed of haste!

So, I were doing an ad for Adidas and I had a dawn of realisation… Rosie who I'd known since she were about eight, I fink, were gonna be me bird. Like *me bird*! I were a bit scared of it, but I fought maybe it were time to have somet steady in me life. I fought It'd be nice to have someone to share the popcorn with. I proper liked Rosie and I knew she liked me. To this day I've never said the 'L' word to her though. I do in t' film but that's just script in't it?

I know I'm right good looking and I dress real good, I've got nice hair and I'm good at sex but I'm not sure what Rosie sees in me. I mean enough to be more than a one-night stand. She really gets me, ya know? And has a great sense of humour. I can take piss out of her all t' time and she just takes it on t' chin.

I had to fly out to Belfast before the rest of the cast which now includes Verne Troyer, as Archimedes, Kevin Bishop from the *Kevin Bishop Show,* as me mate Dougie, and Kelly Brook from naughty calendars, Piranha 3DD and me wet dreams. She were playing herself, just like Rosie from Leeds were as me bird Rosie. Kevin and Verne got on so well Kevin ended up putting his ball sack on Verne's head, can't remember why. But he's a proper wind up is Bishop. Fink I'm meeting him next week for a jar or seven.

As soon as I got there, the airport staff asked me for a photo. Never had that before. Nice for t' ego like. And they were lookers. I went straight for a costume fitting and while having that fitting I called Paul (who'd been out there a couple of weeks and already had a Belfast twang in his voice) and told him we'd gotta meet up in a room and sort the script out. We were staying in right posh apartments next to each other and he said come round to mine.

Aidan, one of t' producers, were in the same block as us. He's a nice Geordie fella. Not so Geordie that ya cudn't tell what he were saying like some of the locals. I remember, before me and Paul got in that room to look at the script, the first Belfastonian that spoke to me said... well, I *fought* he said, 'What has ya hair?'

I said, 'Eh?'

He said, 'What has ya hair?'

I said, 'Me hair has highlights.'

He looked at me confused and Aiden started laffing. 'He said "What has ya here?"'

I said, 'Oh, erm... a plane. A plane has got me 'ere.'

The Belfast man laffed, 'Ah Keet,' he said. 'Ya funny one, so ya are! Can ya talk to me friend on the phone?'

So I spoke to his friend on t' phone. Cudn't really tell what he were saying apart from, 'How d'ya find Belfast? What's the situation?' I told him it seemed nice but I'd just got 'ere and the situation were Nando's! I were off for me dinner!

I did notice they had a lot of tidy birds in Belfast though, which made me wonder if I'd made the right move getting hooked up with Rosie. But I were gonna be there for five and a half weeks and it were either gonna go terribly wrong or not terribly wrong.

The next day me and Paul locked ourselves away in his red hot apartment. He had his heating on full whack, cos he were scared he were gonna fall ill. Ya dingbat,

Paul. And we spent three days and nights rewriting before t' cast arrived. We worked so hard, me brain felt like it were gonna fall out. Now and again Paul'd pop out with me Nando's card and come back with mountains of chicken and we'd get back on it. Me pacing up and down talking and Paul typing away like a mad man, but we did it and were happy with it, although I knew we were gonna change somet once we got on set. It always happens cos ya come up with better ideas when ya shooting.

The day finally came for a table read. Kevin, Verne and Rosie had all arrived, but Kelly hadn't turned up yet and I were worried that she might pull out. I'm not sure why. When I saw her calendar above mine in HMV, I fought maybe that were a good omen. I bought one and took it back to me apartment and totally destroyed it!

Eventually Kelly did turn up and me, Rosie and Kevin, who'd already starred alongside her in a play and knew her, went to meet her. She were smaller than I fought – apart from her bangers, which were a lot biggerer. I kept on clocking Rosie looking at me to see if I were giving Kelly the eye. The fact were, I were! But Rosie weren't skilled enough to see it yet! I were a pro at this. But when Kelly got up to get a round in when we were having a drink at this nice little boozer, I got it in the ear from Rosie.

'I can see you ya know,' she said.

I knew how to play it. 'I can see ya too, and ya look Fit as Flip'. That seemed to keep her quiet for a bit.

The main fing were Kelly Brook were really nice and easy to get on with. I wun't of minded getting on her and all, but I were keeping it all professional like. The fing about Kelly that not many people realise is that she's not fick but she sometimes she just acts it. She's fick in certain areas, her breasts, for example, are very fick. But she's not really fick like a dingbat is fick; it's a cover. I bet she could invent somet like a rocket, I'm not saying she's an engineer but she could meke somet and people would be like, 'who invented that?' and they'd be like 'Oh, that? That were Kelly Brook'. Anywhere the next day I were gonna be banging her. It were in t' script that I wrote.

Doing the film were totally different from doing telly. I remember the first day's shoot had me in what were supposed to be a grubby shit-stinking bedsit in London. It were horrible and cold outside. It were always cold and rainy in Belfast. A nice city, but so fucking cold. The film were supposed to be set in London, but we were shooting it in Belfast cos the production company Generator were based there. Plus, I think it were cheaperer. The people were lovely and we all got on, but it just took ages to do anyfing. I might do a scene where I'd only say four lines and that'd take about two hours. Setting up, lighting... blah-blah-blah-blah.

Been off it for a few weeks. Lots has gone on since I last wrote owt. Been on me mate's stag do, been stalked by a Danish bird and won a little fing called a BAFTA. Cudn't believe it! *Celebrity Juice* were up for two: YouTube Audience Award and Best Entertainment Programme, which went to Derren Brown. Met him a few times and he's a good lad. Right nice wizard. But *Juice* won the

YouTube Audience Award, voted for by t' public so that means a lot. Cudn't believe we beat *Sherlock*. It felt very odd sat there. It felt like we'd sneaked in through t' fire escape.

We met *Doctor Who* and all and asked him if he'd come on *Juice*, so let's wait and see what happens. Fink it'd be good to do a *Dr Who* special, where we're all dressed as different Doctors, even though I know nowt about *Dr Who* really. I'm more into *Back t' Future*. My fancy dress costume of choice. T' kids like *Dr Who* though, don't they? Perhaps rather than do a *Dr Who* special, we could do a sci-fi special, all dressed as different sci-fi characters. Fearne could be Zelda from *Terrahawks*, I could be Han Solo from *Star Wars* or maybe Luke Skywalker as me hair's more like his, Holly could be Super Girl or Jabba the Hutt (she's got the tits for it). I swear her bangers are getting biggerer. I were

FEARNE'S MASSIVE NOSTRILS

watching her on t' telly t'other night on that *Voice* fing and it looked like she'd bought the Mitchell brothers along, lovely Holly Willoughbooby!

Other week I were asked to introduce Jonathan Ross on stage at the Channel 4 Comedy Gala 2012. Personally asked by him and all, which is nice in't it? He were on the last series of *Juice* and were a great guest. He filled in for Fearne while she were on holiday doing some charity fing or other. So of course I did it. I got down t' O2. That's right! The effing massive O2. I saw The Spice Girls there, and Peter Kay. I saw me name on t' poster and I fought, 'Ey up, I must be doing more than just intro-ing Jonathan.' I were watching the other acts on before me and I fought, 'Shit, I'm gonna have to do a turn. A proper turn! I'm not a stand-up!' So Jonathan Ross comes out and I said, 'I fought I were just introducing ya, I'm not a stand-up. I've got no material'.

He said, 'Just go out there and talk, you'll be alwight.'

So I fought, 'Fuck Keith! Just go out there and talk. I can talk!' Yeah, I can talk me! So I went out there and talked. I even got to cop a feel of a ladies boob. Said to her that me mate works at NASA at t' weekend and he's been doing an experiment to see what's more common – the left tit or the right to be the biggest? Said I believe it were the left and it hangs lower. So I copped a feel. I say give it try: if ya own a pair have a go and if you're a man just ask politely. It dint work with Holly Willoughbooby when I tried it with 'er at V, but if at first ya don't succeed try, try, try again...

195

Filming me film

It **were the first day on set** with t' lady of dreams, Miss Kelly Brook. In the scene that I were doing, I were gonna be vigorously snogging her mouth then pushing her to the ground to smash her back doors in. Romantic like! I were a bit nervous to be honest, but how hard were it gonna be? Not hard at all hopefully! If I'd have got a hard on, I fink I would've got a bit embarrassed, but this were Kelly Brook. So, I practised the scene with the director first, then just put him in me mind when I were doing it with Kelly.

I always fink honesty is the best policy, so I just had it out with her. I said 'Kelly, has anyone ever got a straight on when they've been doing a naughty scene with ya?'

She said, 'A straight on?'

I said 'Yeah, ya know – a stiffy, a lob on, a bonk on, a hard prick?'

She told me that they all do and she'd be offended if they dint. Well she were gonna be offended by me then cos I made it me mission not to get a rocket in me pocket. Just wanted to be professional like. So I kept the director in mind when I were Parrot Tonguing Kelly. That were the name I give me kissing method with Kelly – The Parrot Tongue.

I kissed Rosie in the film, which were odd, cos it were a real kiss but we were acting. Of course, I'd kissed 'er nuff times in real life but this were in front of t' cameras and t'were proper odd. It just felt like we were opening and closing our mouths right close. I got a bit of a stiffy then, but I were allowed to with me bird. Still it were a little embarrassing in front of t' crew.

The next scene I were doing with Kelly were a right naughty scene. We were stripping off in front of each other and having a kind of flirt off. When she took her bra top fing off, it were pretty difficult to keep looking into her eyes even though she has lovely eyes. She's got equally lovely bangers! In scene it played in the film after the part where I've had a penis extension and I cudn't control me willy so a large amount of man milk squirts out when I get a bit excited. There were gallons of it. Of course it weren't real man milk. It were a mixture of water and egg white. Looked real enough though. Paul the Director were sat beneath me on t' floor pumping it up into me face from a big canister. We only had time to do it once so we cun't laff. And that were me first day shooting with Kelly. I just hoped she'd come back the next day. Luckily she did.

I fink that night were the night we all went out with t' crew. Rosie dint come out. I cudn't remember why, but we were getting on great and I were enjoying having a proper bird. Sex on tap – that's proper love I guess. I fink Rosie knew how well it were going between us so she dint mind me going out with Kelly, who, by the way, drinks like a fish and eats like Geoff Capes. Boy, can she put it away. Fair play to her. I hate women that fuss about their weight all t' time. Ya know the type that's constantly living off a salad and always down the gym. Apart from Rosie, of course.

Talking of Rosie, well some of the bits in the film are based on truth. Rosie says that she likes me cos I meke her smile. And I like meking 'er smile, mekes me feel right big in me heart. By that's soft as fuck, I know. Sexually she's me equivalent. She gives a great blow job and lets me seagull her bangers. Although she don't let me go in t' back doors. I'm always saying I'd smash those back doors in. The fact is I've only ever gone in a few people's back doors but I'm not gonna name any names.

I can remember when I asked Rosie if she'd ever got on t' tube and gone in an entrance where it says 'no entrance'. She dint really get me analogy and as she'd not really been on t' tube, she dint know what I were talking about. So I had to spell it out. I just said to her 'Would ya ever do it up t' arse'? This is where Rosie is clever. She said, 'Why? D'ya wanna do it up t' arse'?

I said not really. She's too sweet for that. Like I said it's naughty. When she asked me if I'd ever done it up t' arse, I just told her that I cudn't remember.

Changing the subject, there's one scene in t' film where I get mugged. This is the turning point in t' film where it switches to fantasy. I wanted this scene to be really dark and shocking. I spent two days on t' floor of a dirty, cold subway getting beaten up. When we got into t' edit with it though, it were just a bit too dark. We weren't meking *Kidulthood*, we were were meking a comedy about me origins.

Anywhere, I've got the best guy ever in t' film. Me dad, Billie Ocean! I know ya fink I'm joking but me mam says she had a fun time with him years ago at a gig and I never knew if she were joking. I like the idea of him being me dad. When I met him, we got on like an 'ouse on fire! He were a lovely, lovely man. He performed 'When the Going Gets Tough' on set and the atmosphere were ace! Everyone loved him. Avid Merrion were there from *Bo' Selecta*. He described Billy as a black Santa Claus. In't that a great idea! A black Santa Claus. I love the idea that Santa is a black rasta! Wun't that do great fings for equality? Same with James Bond. Wun't it be good if Will Smith were James Bond?! Or me! I'm part black if me mam's telling t' truth.

It were great to have Holly and Fearne in t' film too. It were lovely of them to come over to Belfast. I'd missed them both. I fink when Rosie saw me with Fearne though she fought maybe there were somet going on. The fact is we're good mates, that's all. I give her loads of abuse, pecifically about her massive nostrils, but we like each other really. I fink Rosie is a wee bit worried that we like each other a bit *too* much.

Lots of people featured in the film in the end – lots of me mates and it were a bit like *Juice*: Rizzle Kicks, Tinchy, Jedward, the Hoff (oh my god! Knight Rider! Can't believe I've done a film with him!), Denise Van Outen, me mate Bunton and Mel C and Gary Barlow. He's definitely one of me heros. He texted me while I were out there and asked me if I wanted to come to his gig he were doing. I said I were busy meking me own film, but asked him if he'd like to meke a little appearance in it. He said he would if he were around. Now people sometimes say that when they actually mean 'no', so I were right chuffed when the day came and we had him on set. He's a lovely fella. If I were hormone sexual I'd wank him defo.

Chris Moyles also did a bit for us, and Peter Andre, Jason Donovan, me mate Gino and me old pal Paddy McGuinness. I say 'old' but he's not really old, same age

as me I fink. Paddy played
'Gary Apple', me cousin.

There were a lot of pissing
about with Paddy being in
t' film, but if we'd had more
time he'd have been in it
more. It were all to do with
schedules. He's so busy.
Next time if we do a sequel,
*Keith Lemon: The Film 2, The
Sequel*, he'll be in it more.

Belfast were great too –
everyfing were 10 minutes away and t' people were
lovely but it were nice to come home for Christmas.
I love Christmas. I fink Christmas dinner and Chinese
are me favourite foods.

Fink round about then I were doing more promotion
stuff. I met Stella McCartney. She designed the
Olympic uniform. She were nice. I would've banged
her. She were sexy for a ginger! Everyone were walking
on egg shells around her but at the end of the day we
all take a shit, don't we? Just approach people with
a friendly smile and good manners and that's all ya
need. And that's all I did. Talked about finger blasting
with her a little bit too and she loved it. She had a dirty
twinkle in her eye!

Anywhere, after spending lots of quality time with
Rosie doing the film and over Christmas, I fought it
would be nice to take her on t' red carpet with me – kind
of meking me and her official. So we went to NTAs
together. A few people said that I were punching above
me weight a bit with Rosie. I told them to 'Fuck off!'

Hey I'm good looking me, ya know! And I'm great at sex! She always sticks up for me does Rosie, tells people I'm not 'ginger' but strawberry blond and that I'm not punching above me weight cos scientifically I'm better looking than her. Proportionally me eyes are more centrific than hers. They're more equal apart than hers. And one of hers is a bit lazy. And she's got a large forehead. But it all works together as a unit, meking her the fittest girl at the NTAs that night. Fitter even than anyone from *Hollyoaks* or even Michelle Keegan. I were proud to have her on me arm. And the dress that I bought her that cost £45 in t' sale looked like it cost £145!

It were a really busy time of year and I were asked to present *The BRITs Red Carpet* show and the after party show on ITV2 with Laura Whitmore. I had the time of me life and just got drunk and had a good crack with Laura. She's right nice.

But the highlight of the night had to be meeting Kylie. I were overwhelmed. Cudn't believe she actually knew who I were. She came over and said 'Give me a cuddle. I'm freezing!' I'd have given 'er more than a cuddle. I din't want pull away when I pulled away from the cuddle because I'd thought they'd have to blur it out what were going on downstairs. She looked fit as chuff. Right small she is. A proper little spinner. I met Jessie J, too, who I'd recently developed a fancy for after having a mucky dream about 'er. Funny in't it, when ya have a mucky dream about someone and then ya fancy them t' next day. But to have a mucky dream and then actually *meet* them t' next day. Madness! It were good to see Noel Gallagher. Met him in a toilet years ago. Cool bastard he is. His brother Liam is cool too. Fink they should get back together like Spice Girls did or East 17. Dint go so well for East 17 though. Did they get back together?

Maybe they dint. Steps did though, dint they? Lovely Claire. She's still really pretty. Especially when she does that little rabbit nose fing that Bunton use to do as well. Right cute. Yeah it were a great night.

Fit as chuff

Dream meKer

In between all this madness, I started to film me new show *Lemonaid*. The idea of the show were to help all those people who were vexed by demolishing their problems and meking their dreams come true. I loved doing *Lemonaid*. It were a nice team and Sarah the producer were brilliant. Top lass. Fink she's pregnant now. Probably had it by now. I hope it's not strawberry blond. The first VT (that's short for videotape) we did, which were for the pilot, were in Bolton with a little kid called Liam, who wanted to be me for t' day. The show were like a mix of *Jim'll Fix it* and *Surprise Surprise*. The people on it were kinda nominated or put forward by a friend or family member. Should've seen t' look on t' little lad's face when he saw me standing there. I fought he'd shit a brick. If ya'd watched it then ya saw it. Ya wun't have seen his mam there eyein me up. I'm sure she wanted a piece of me Lemon, she did!

I felt a bit bad though cos I must've stunk of drink. I went around Paddy McGuinness' gaff with Dan, the executive producer, t' night before. Well we were shooting in Bolton and it felt only right that we pop round and see Paddy as he lives there. Between the three of us, we polished off three or four bottles of vodka. I can remember sitting there, watching MTV while Dan and Paddy were wrestling on the floor. All I could hear were glasses being broke. Cudn't remember getting back to the hotel. But the next day Paddy said we'd left his house smelling like Yates's winebar. He said he had us on CCTV footage trying to get into our cab. We cudn't walk; we were totally twatted... I can tell ya. I felt like I had two Jack Russells fighting in me belly.

I remember we were shooting with the DeLorean car from *Back t' Future*. I had to tell the man whose car it were (Steve) to pull over cos I fought I were gonna chuck up. Oooosh! I were rough that day. But I got through and it made for a good VT.

The Wedding VT were a good one, too. We stayed over night in a Premier Inn, I fink. No sign of Lenny Henry though. Use to love him when he use to say 'Ooooo oooooooooooooKaaaaaaaaaaaaaay!'. The good fing about the Premier Inn (or Holiday Inn or Travel Lodge, can't remember which one it were) were the fantastic interiors. The toilet is positioned so that if ya sit with the door open, ya can see the telly perfectly. Ya can watch shite, while meking shite. I watched the whole of *Jeremy Kyle* on t' toilet before me surprise attendance at that wedding.

What happened were, the best man had got in touch with the researchers (I called them The Dream Team) and asked if I'd come. He were told I cudn't meke it and then... I made it! We hid in a backroom for ages being really quiet. I remember taking a picture of our lunch all laid on a blanket finking, 'While they're all enjoyed wedding cake and such, we're gonna be eating sandwiches and Scotch eggs.' I like Scotch eggs mind. So just as the best man is about to hand the rings over I jumped out. Weren't sure what kind of reception I were gonna get. Maybe, 'Get out of our effing wedding ya dingbat, can't ya see you're spoiling our day'. But t'were total opposite! Were a great response and even tears. I'd flown over their friends from Australia, paid for t' flight and everyfing. They were over t' moon. It were all about meking dreams come true after all. We got outta there before everyone started to get pissed. Otherwise all women start fingering me arse. But it wasn't all big gestures, it were the simple things in life too. One woman's glasses kept falling off her head so I sellotaped them on and sorted her right out. Rachel who were part of the team were a lovely lass, she did a great job of finding all t' people I'd be Lemonaiding. I would've had a go on her as she were fit. Looked like Jennifer Aniston, from behind. In fact she were Jennifer Aniston's body double in a film! Dint 'arf look like her from t' back.

The studio stuff were ace too. The set were amazing. The desk were me face. Every Saturday tea time there I were on t' telly sat on me own face. Each week we had different celebrity helpers, helping me *Lemonaid* the studio. We had Cilla Black on and got on great with her. Holly told me to treat her like a Queen and she'd be lovely. Weren't 'ard though as I treat all women like they're Queens. Right liked Cilla. Then we had Mark Wright from *TOWIE*. Really nice bloke, just cun't hold his smile long enough till the ad break. He'll pick it up. Lovely man. Caught him just looking down at his arms, admiring his own biceps and I said 'Look at ya looking at ya arms. D'ya want a look at mine? Ya can count me freckles.' Nice fella, got good hair, but his clothes look too small for him. Guess that's his style.

We also had on the beautiful Michelle Keegan. She's got the best skin in telly, flawless her skin. Not sure what she uses.

We also had Peter Andre. The loveliest dingbat on telly. No matter what ya fink of Peter, he is a top bloke. Shite at telling jokes but he's a lovely man and a great sport. Would go for a pint with him any day. In fact we keep talking about it, but never arrange owt. For years I fought his hair were made out of tar. But it's actually real!

Me good mate Bunton did the pilot for *Lemonaid*.
Love doing stuff with Emma. It's just like being at work
with ya mate. I'm very lucky. When ya working on telly
with ya mates ya can go that little bit further cos they
know it's all just a joke. I remember putting me knob in
Emma's mouth and I got away with it cos I said I were
joking! I dint mean to put it in and it were just a joke. By
the way, I dint really! But I did lick her tongue. Might
as well tell you I'd put me knob in and all. Might have
ruined our friendship though if I'd done that, I guess.

And finally we had Louis Walsh. By he's good crack.
He's a great sport too. First fing he'll say is 'Say
whatever ya want to me, take the piss I don't care'. He
always says I should come over to Ireland. Louis, if ya
reading this, let me know when? I'd love to meet Bono
or Nadine from Girls Aloud. Actually I've met her.
Stunning, she is. Could do with putting a bit of timber
on though, but Bang Tidy! We had The Saturdays on
t' last episode and all. All F.A.F. I wonder if they all
sexually experiment with each other when they're on
tour. Nice fought in't it? Lovely girls. Cudn't tell ya
which one is me favourite though. I'd smash all t' back
doors in. Balls deep!

It were a great show and we gave some amazing prizes
away, iPads, cars, holidays. Sometimes I were a bit jealous.

But it were dead nice giving stuff away, I felt right
good, like I were meking a difference to people's lives.
Sometimes though I were a bit scared that me heart
were gonna get too big for me chest. I remember a bit
that weren't in t' show with this young lad who were
about 21, so not much youngerer than me and he'd just
graduated from 'uni', whatever that is, and he cudn't
tie a tie. Who knows what he'd been doing all his life.
Anywhere, I said to him that Michelle Keegan use to
work at *Tie Rack* and she were gonna teach him how to
tie a tie in t' ad break. If he learnt how to do that when
we came back I'd give him a tie-related prize! He did it
and guess what we gave him? A trip to the place where
ties were invented, that's right Thailand! The lucky
bastard! And we dint even use that bit in t' show. We
could've just took the prize back off him. But it weren't
about that. It were about fixing people's problems and
meking dreams come true. To show just how nice I am.
Cos I am ya know I'm nice, on a par with Cheryl Cole
when she went to see t' troops.

I have to admit it's great meking telly and films.
Sometimes I wake up and I fink 'How the eff...?' Then I'll
go have a shit and wank in t' shower and I'll go have fun
all day, whether its doing *Juice* with Holly and Fearne
or rolling around with Kelly Brook for t' film. It were
insane going to Cannes to promote the film with 'er. I
remember being interviewed, glass of wine in me hand,
which, by the way, were never empty. Soon as it started
to go down they'd fill it up. I'm looking out over Cannes,
where all 't boats are and I fought, 'Jesus on a bike. If me
Leeds massive could see me now.'

In fact, I nearly dint meke it there, I picked up the
wrong passport. Had Rosie's instead of me own. They
all look t' same. I missed Rosie a bit while I were out

there though. By now me and her were a proper 'un, an official item! We'd even started filming a reality show called *Lemon La Vida Loca*. At first it were a bit strange with t' cameras in ya face all t' time. Cudn't even take a shite without a cameraman stood in t' corner, but if it's hard for me, I fink it's all probably harder for Rosie. And as serious as we are, I still have a wandering eye.

We were filming the reality show fing other night and we had Jenny Powell over. Her from competition VTs on *This morning* or *Day Break*. She asks fings such as: 'Which children's TV presenter has a puppet called Edd the Duck?

'Is the answer
A) Metal
B) Wood
 or C) Andi Peters

Anywhere, I were having a little flirt with her and it may have led to a little kiss. Nowt serious. I wun't do owt to hurt Rosie, I'm just a bit emotionally immature sometimes, apparently. It's an adjustment period for me I guess. Me tally wacker in't just mine to get it out and do what I want with it anymore. It's somet I share with Rosie and I've gotta respect it and her more.

If I don't see you through week...

This whole past few years have been a crazy journey that hopefully is gonna continue. This reality show fing comes out soon and hopefully people will like that and we'll do more. Its probably been out and gone now. Hope ya liked it. The films gonna be out soon and that is just total madness. *Keith Lemon: The Film*. Total effing madness. Cun't believe I made a film. I'm a bit bamboozled by it all to be honest. I were in Nando's today with me stylist Heather talking about what I'm gonna wear for t' premiere. Somet white with feathers, flash as fuck, I fink! I don't dress that mad when I'm just popping down t' Costcos. But for telly and what have ya I like to jazz it up a bit. Cudn't wear some of t' stuff I wear on telly in t' street, I'd get bricked.

So yeah, I fink I'm up to date with where I am in me life now. Gotta hand this in soon. It's been very ferapeutic looking back. Maybe I'll write another in a few years when I've done more stuff, if I'm still on t' telly. I hope I am cos it's a great job. I have such a good time and I meet great people. Who can say that 89% of the people they work with they'd actually have it off with? I can say that cos most of the people I work with are Fit as Flip!

So, I've got another series of *Juice* in September, and me film and me reality show fing. Who knows what the future holds. I expect one day I'll be married with kids. Mini Me Keith. I have them in t' film but that's just a film. I'd like to do another *World Tour* as that were good fun and I'd definitely like to do more films.

I'll do *Celebrity Juice* as long as Holly and Fearne are there. Imagine if we're still doing it when we're old farts. Holly's tits will be round her knees! Fuck knows what Fearne will look like. I suppose I'll look good – as men just get better looking with age, don't they? Well most men. I wonder what Michael Jackson would've looked like as an old man? What would the Moonwalk have looked like performed with a zimmer? Strange how fings turn out. But it's been a great ride and as me friend's mam use to say, 'If I dint see ya through week, I'll see ya through t' winda.' Ooooshhhhhhhhhhhhhhhhhhhhhhhh!

All t' best. Lots of love, Keith xxx

Dirty Prancing

Script Draft

[Show starts with a black screen, we hear Keith and Paddy (V.O.) discussing the film they're going to spoof.]

KEITH [V.O.]

I always saw meself as a bit of a Patrick Swayze.

PADDY [V.O.]

What's my name?

KEITH [V.O.]

Paddy?

PADDY

Which is short for?

KEITH

Patrick.

PADDY

That's why I'm Swayze and you're gonna be 'Babby'.

KEITH

But I've got a tash...

PADDY

That's not all you've got, but we'll have to make do. So strap it up
and press 'Record', flower!

[We cut to black-and-white footage of old people dancing in slow
mo.]

[On screen graphics appear.]

'DIRTY PRANCING'

[Cut to Keith dressed as a young woman (Babby) in the back of a
Ford Mondeo. It's towing a four-berth caravan. Music is playing
in the background as we hear Keith's V.O.]

BABBY [V.O.]

It was the summer of 2007 and we where off on our jollydays.
Everyone called me 'Babby' and it didn't occur to me to mind.
although I did mind a bit, but not enough for it to occur to me. That
was before Joe Swash won 'I'm a Celebrity Get Me Out of Here!',
Fern Britton was slim and I couldn't wait to join the mounted
polioo. I novor thought I'd find a guy as great as my dad.

[Keith leans forward to wrap his arms around his dad, who is
driving. His dad is sipping on a can of Tenants and smiling as he
gives a wink back through the rear view mirror. Babby's sister,
Lisa, is also sat in the car looking miserable combing her hair.
We cut to a sign on the side of the road, 'Jellymans Mountain
Retreat'.]

That was the summer we went to Jellymans.

[The car pulls into the resort, people mingling, lots of hustle and bustle, loads of rows of caravans and tents. A fat bloke is walking around shouting into a loud haler.]

FAT BLOKE

Welcome, welcome cockers. Hurry up and unpack folks, the first round of the knobbly forearms contest is about to commence in the Fred West suite!

[Babby and her family are getting out of the car and starting to unpack. Max Jellyman spots them.]

MAX

Doc, great to see you up here at long last.

BABBY [V.O.]

Everyone called me dad, 'Doc'. He wasn't a medical doctor, but in fact a travelling salesman for the shoe company Dr Martins, which where very popular with the skin heads of the 60s and 70s.

DAD

Max! How are those feet?

MAX [to Babby's family]

If it wasn't for this man I'd be in a wheelchair now. I was a slave to my bunions but the Doc here got me a pair of 18-hole lace-ups [He lifts up trouser leg to reveal bright red Dr Martins] and now life's good. I kept the best caravan for you and your girls.

LISA

Shit! I've left my trainers at home!

MUM

Language, Lisa!

LISA

That was English. I can say it in French if you like.

Merde, j'ai quitté mon formateurs à la maison.
[English subtitles].

DAD

This is not a tragedy. A tragedy is three men trapped in a mine or police dogs used in Birmingham.

LISA

What you on about?

BABBY

Or a dog with no legs that's had to have skateboard wheels grafted to its stumps to enable it to manoeuvre to and fro.

LISA

I don't know what you two have been smoking. But I's gotta get me some of that shi –

MUM

Lisa!

LISA

Merde!
['Shit' subtitled].

BABBY

I didn't know you could speak French.

LISA

I can't. I got a translator on my iPhone, in't it.

[Young ginger bloke approahes Babby.]

GINGER BLOKE

Hey! Later on there's a 'bring a watermelon' party up at the club house. Dirty dancing and everything! It's gonna be proper! But don't tell your parents!

[Cut ext. night shot of caravan.]

BABBY

Mum, Dad I'm just going out for a look around.

[Cut to int. of caravan.]

DAD

Babby, are those watermelons down your top?

BABBY

No they're my bangers!

LISA

Dad, man you're sick! Checking out Babby's bangers. Banger checker-outerer!

MUM

Were you just checking out Babby's bangers?

DAD

No, I thought they were watermelons. I heard there was a 'bring a watermelon' party at the club house. I don't want her up there. I know what goes on there. Dirty dancing and all sorts. Checking out her bangers? What do you take me for, some kind of pervert?

[Dad sits down sips on his tenants super and lifts up a dirty mag called 'Big Bangers'.]

[Cut to Babby running up to the clubhouse. Cut to her at the doorway as it opens to everyone dirty dancing. She walks in and spots Jonny (Paddy), who is dancing with a pregnant girl. He spots her. Their eyes lock. There's an instant attraction.]

JONNY [to girl]

Stay there.

GIRL [Maria]

Jonny!

JONNY

Button it!

[Jonny dances his way over to Babby.]

JONNY

How do?

BABBY

Ey-up! I brought some watermelons.

JONNY [disappointed]

Oh! For a minute there I thought they were your cheeky pippins. I were gonna say... Look, pop your melons down there with the rest of 'em, and why don't me and you have a dance?

[Babby puts the watermelons down on a pile of other watermelons and starts dancing with Jonny.]

BABBY

What about your bird?

JONNY

That in't me bird, it's me dance partner that I work with her on t' holiday camp.

BABBY

Is she up the duff?

JONNY

Aye. But we're getting rid. She puts it about a bit and we don't know who the father is. It in't mine, if that's what ya thinking. I fed her horse but that were it. I didn't give her me carrot, if you know what I mean.

BABBY

No, I don't know what ya mean.

JONNY

Like I said, she's just me dance partner.

BABBY

I din't think she'd be able to dance in her condition.

JONNY

Your right. It's like dancing with a whale. Fancy filling in for her? We do a big show at the end of the week for all t' holiday camp.

BABBY

Me? I can't even dance the Macarena.

JONNY

Don't worry. I once taught Steven Hawkins how to do the Moonwalk and he's never looked back!

BABBY

That's amazing. I think I'm falling in love with you.

JONNY

Slow down Babby! I've not even given you the plumbers wipe yet.

[He spits into his cupped hand while doing a miming motion.]

[Cut to next day.]

[Jonny is teaching Babby how to dance. Close up of their feet, Babby stands on Jonny's feet.]

JONNY

Oh god! Me in-grown toenail. Jesus tonight! Don't step on the two. You've gotta start on the two. Find the two, kapeesh?

BABBY

Well, actually no I don't. I don't understand the whole number thing. Ya see when I dance I go 'de-de-de, de-de-de'. I don't count.

JONNY

Is she tapped or what?

BABBY

Well I'm 47% dyslexic actually.

JONNY

Alright then Rain Man... Woman, let's go again. I'll go slow.

It's One, two, three. One, two, three. You don't start dancing till the two.

[Cut to montage of them both dancing. Babby is rubbish but progressively gets better.]

JONNY

The steps aren't enough. Feel the music.

[More dancing montage.]
JONNY

Let me try something.

[He takes Babby's hand and puts it on his chest.]
Ga-gun, ga-gun, ga-gun. Feel the music. And one, two, three. One two, three.

BABBY

De-de-de, de-de-de–

JONNY

FOUR, THREE, FOUR, THREE.

BABBY

I still don't understand. But, yeah, I can feel the music.

[Cut to ext shot of Jonny's caravan. Babby is running towards it. She enters, cut to int. shot. They're still practising dancing.]

JONNY

This is my dance space. This is your dance space. I don't go into your dance space, you don't go into mine. Friggin 'ell come on, Spaghetti arms.

BABBY

That's pretty harsh! If anyone's got spaghetti arms, its you. Your arms are longer than mine. Bleeding Mr Tickle! Your hands are all over the place trying to cop a feel of me boobs.

[They keep dancing.]

BABBY

I feel sick. Can we take a break?

JONNY

Your not preggers are ya?

BABBY

No, that's her, and I feel a bit weird with her here watching.

JONNY

Are you saying I'm the dad again?

BABBY

No! But you've fed her horse.

MARIA

Look Jonny, why don't I have a go with her?

[Both Babby and and Maria start dancing. Jonny sits down and watches.]

JONNY

Oooo, lez be friends!

[He grabs a box of Kleenex.]

MARIA

Right, I think she's got it. Why don't you practise the lift in t' paddling pool?

JONNY

Fair dos.

[Cut to Jonny and Babby outside practising the lift in a large paddling pool outside the caravan. After a few attempts they get it.]

BABBY

Yes, we've got it!

JONNY

Be better if you could get your arms out. [Under breath] And have a shave...

BABBY

Not happening!

JONNY

Bollocks.

BABBY

I love you, ya know.

JONNY

Behave, I told ya. I've not even shagged ya yet. Come on then let's go make love while ad breaks on.

BABBY

Oh Jonny!

JONNY

Lye darn, am bart fuck thee! [spits on hand].

END OF PART ONE

WELL, THAT'S JUST A TEASE! IF IT MADE YA MOIST FOR MORE AND YOU'D LIKE T' SEE IT ON TELLY, THEN START A PETITION FINGY TO THOSE LOVELY PEOPLE AT ITV...ADDRESS IT TO PETER FINNYGAN, ANGIE WAYNE OR CLAIRE ZOLTAN!

FanKs

Just like to say a few fanks to:
Everyone on Twittor apart from t' rude people.
They can go fuck themselves with a bag of nettles.

T' Facebook people for all t' support although I don' t go
on it as much now cos its so depressing seeing girls from
school that were once fit have now let themselves go.

All t' woman I've had that have made me the spectacular
lover that I am today. Even to the ones that gave me
STDs. It helped me develop me character.

All me friends and family for putting up with me and
being there when I've needed ya the most. Like when I
fell of a wall drunk having a piss and cut me knob and
Paul took me to t' hospital. Fink that's what happened?
Or did Paul cut his knob? Thanks anyway, Paul.

Phil and Shaun, me Leeds mates, for doing great music
for the shows I've done. I got you a job so you owe me
a drink!

Me mam for everyfing. I wun't be hear if it weren't for
you. It were you that give me me beautiful strawberry
blond locks. Ya must be so proud of me. But not as much
as I am of you.

Julie who makes me hair strawberry blond. I fink it's a
bit longerer on one side though.

Peter, Elaine, Angela and Claire at ITV for giving me a
job in telly. Is there any chance I can have more holidays?

Or another show where I go on holiday and it's filmed for your channel?

The production companies I've worked with, cos its you guys that actually meck the shows and I just talk a lot. But without me you'd have no job. So like me mates Phil and Shaun, you owe me a drink too.

Big ups to Dan, Leon and Ed. Love you guys but not in a hormone sexual way. Even though you'd like it to be.

Spencer, Ben, James, Pete, Joe, Roy. Old times! One day we'll play silly buggers again hopefully.

George and Lara at James Grant Management and everyone else there, you've been brilliant! And honestly George and Lara if you ever want to have an orgy I'm up for it (if Rosie is ok with it).

All t' people that have been guests on whatever show it is I've been doing. I hope I've never offended ya in any way. Especially Craig David, I hope we can hang out one day and ya can buy me a beer.

Jane and everyone at Orion Books for letting me make a book. Next time can I have one of those ghostwriters? I'm slow as fuck at typing and that's why its taken so long.

All t' photographers I've worked with that have made me look Bang Tidy. Especially David, ya clumsy bastard.

The special lady in me life that keeps me in toe. Is that a real sentence? Not sure what being kept in toe actually means. But seriously I cun't have done it without you. They say behind every great man there is a great woman behind them. And I fank you for being great but mostly fank you for letting me behind you! I like it that way better so I can't smell ya morning breath. I've enjoyed sharing me with you and hope you've enjoyed me as much as I've enjoyed you. 'Ere's to us. Let's raise a glass and cheers and look into our eyes. Apparently if ya cheers and don't look into their eyes you have seven years bad sex. But that's hardly gonna happen if you're still shacked up with me. Cos 'sex' is me middle name. Well it in't actually, it's 'Ian', but ya know what I mean.

If I've missed anyone out, I am deeply sorry. But I honestly appreciate everyone I've come across. And all t' people I've met. You may not know it, but you've probably influenced me in some way. So in some way, you are responsible for some of the fings I may have said that I shun't of said. But I forgive you. It's not you, it's me. I'm very easily influenced. Fank you so much for everyfing, even if you just shouted 'sha-ting' or 'potato' at me in the street. It's a sign that you care. Without you I don't exist. Well I do, but it just means if you're not watching me on t' telly, there's no ratings and then I'll have to get a proper job, or go back to selling Securipoles.

Remember we are all Bang Tidy in our own special way. No matter what people tell ya. Words can't put you down. You are Bang Tidy in every single way! We are the voice of a new generation. Let's look at the man in the mirror and make that change. Free Melson Nandella. Much love. Peace Off!

Oooosh!

X

I love dressing up as you can see from me film nights with Rosie, so we ran a competition fingy through Twittor and asked you to send in your pics dressed as me! Fanks for all the entries. These were some of me favourites:

PAUL'S DOG

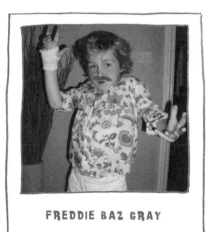

FREDDIE BAZ GRAY

KERRY PATERSON'S SON FINLEY

JOHN BLAKEY

DECLAN MOORE

LUKE CONNOLLY'S MUM
JULIE

FLORENCE HOWEY

Text copyright © Leigh Francis 2012
Dirty Prancing script written in 2010, copyright © Leigh Francis &
Paddy McGuinness

This edition first published in Great Britain in 2012 by
Orion Books, an imprint of the Orion Publishing Group Ltd
Orion House, 5 Upper St Martin's Lane,
London WC2H 9EA
An Hachette UK Company

5 7 9 10 8 6 4

A CIP catalogue record for this book is available
from the British Library.

ISBN: 978 1 4091 4477 9

Designer: Smith & Gilmour
Character illustrations: Leigh Francis

PICTURE CREDITS
Getty Images: 10, 11, 12, 17, 21, 23, 25, 38 (right), 47, 54, 83, 98, 104, 128, 138, 165, 181,
186-187, 190, 196; Rex Features: 24, 35, 114, 182; Andrew Hayes-Watkins: 8-9, 26, 31, 34,
38 (left), 57, 162, 211, 214, 247; Richard Chambury/RichFoto.com: 147, 151, 152, 164.
All other photographs author's own.

Printed in Spain by Cayfosa

The Orion Publishing Group's policy is to use papers that are natural, renewable
and recyclable and made from wood grown in sustainable forests. The logging
and manufacturing processes are expected to conform to the environmental
regulations of the country of origin.

www.orionbooks.co.uk

This book is
dedicated to the
Francis Household